Back to Basics

DISCIPLINE

A Program to Raise Extraordinary Children

Janet Campbell Matson

Bee Good Books
Thousand Oaks, CA

Although the author and publisher have made every effort to ensure the accuracy and completeness of information contained in this book, we assume no responsibility for errors, inaccuracies, omissions, or any inconsistency herein. Any slights of people, places, or organizations are unintentional.

First printing 2004

ISBN 0-9740312-3-2
LCCN 2003104858

ATTENTION CORPORATIONS, UNIVERSITIES, COLLEGES, AND PROFESSIONAL ORGANIZATIONS: Quantity discounts are available on bulk purchases of this book for educational, gift purposes, or as premiums for increasing magazine subscriptions or renewals. Special books or book excerpts can also be created to fit specific needs. For information, please contact Bee Good Books, 2060-D Avenida Los Arboles, #338, Thousand Oaks, CA 91362; (805) 523-9652.

TABLE OF CONTENTS

Rule Three—Don't Delay
Rule Four—Never Punish When You're Angry
Rule Five—Always Follow Through With a Threat
Rule Six—Never Apologize, Explain or Negotiate
Rule Seven—Maintain a United Front
Make it Count

5 Absolute No-Nos

The Fourth Essential Element in Back to Basics Discipline
Disobedience
Disrespect
Temper
Dishonesty
Aggression
Mishaps and House Rules
Stay Focused on the Big Picture

6 Separate Worlds

The Fifth Essential Element in Back to Basics Discipline
What Are They Seeing and Hearing?
Rules Which Separate the Kids From the Adults
Decision Making
Your Space—Your Stuff
Preserving Childhood

7 Sibling Relationships

The Sixth Essential Element in Back to Basics Discipline
Age Has Privilege
Are They Really Twins?
Sibling Cruelty
Tag Alongs
Tattle Tales
Right to Privacy
A Happy Family

8 Home Environment

The Seventh Essential Element in Back to Basics Discipline
Make Them Your Priority and Make Sure They Know It
Routine
Role Modeling
Moral Values

Dinnertime
Great Expectations
The Power of Your Smile
Negative Images
Keep Disagreements Private
Your Home is Your Nest

DEDICATION

To my mother, Jean Campbell, without whom this book would never have been written. Thanks, Mom, for passing along to me the secrets of raising good children. I love you so much.

ACKNOWLEDGMENTS

Special thanks to my daughter, Jeanine Barkan, my partner in the idea which has become this book. We spent many summer days discussing raising children and the importance of discipline. One such afternoon, sipping iced tea and soaking our feet in the pool, we toyed with putting it all in writing. During the months I spent writing this book, Jeanine not only gave me endless support and encouragement, she also gave birth to her second son while raising a toddler from the age of 18 months to two years. As she was reading my rough drafts, she was learning and implementing Back to Basics discipline with her oldest son, Nathan. As she provided him love and security through discipline, we witnessed positive changes in Nathan. Jeanine became an enthusiastic advocate of Back to Basics discipline through her practical experience, and her feedback throughout the process was invaluable to me.

Warm thanks to Julia Melito and Becky Lareau, two mothers who took time out of their busy schedules to read raw, unedited manuscripts and give me their candid feedback.

Thanks to my daughter, April Matson for her assistance in rough draft editing and grammatical correction. Somewhere deep inside her lives an English professor.

And thanks to Janette Haskell and Ken Matson, my daughter and son, for their encouragement, love and support.

Last but absolutely not least, thanks to my husband, John Matson—a model husband and father—who was my partner in raising the best children anyone could imagine.

My husband, John, and I raised four extraordinary children. Today, our son and three daughters are young adults. They are confident, happy and in the process of taking on the world. They are as beautiful inside as they are outside. Each of them is unique and wonderful. They are compassionate, intelligent, responsible and a joy to be around.

Now that our children are grown, we have much to look forward to. As we look to the future, we also reflect on the past 30 years we devoted to raising our children. We made a conscious decision—and thank God we discussed this topic before we had them—we would raise great kids. We made a lot of decisions together during 32 years of marriage, some good and some not so good. Jeanine, Ken, Janette and April are living proof this was the best decision we ever made.

Our parents believed in the importance of discipline, and so did we. John and I agreed on a game plan. The game plan included our pledge for a "united front." No matter what, we would back each other up when disciplining the kids.

There is a bit more to all of this than simply understanding the importance of discipline. I credit my mother for passing along to me the rules for which disciplining children should be applied. She emphasized administering "equal amounts of love and discipline." *Equal* amounts of love and discipline—stressing discipline is just as important and carries just as much weight as hugs, kisses and praise for your children.

I admit I don't have a degree in child psychology. What I *do* have is a terrific success story in raising great kids. They did not just turn out great in the end. They were well-behaved children, good students, trustworthy teenagers and are now extraordinary adults. This book is for them. May they carry on the tradition of raising great kids.

If you are interested in raising extraordinary children, this book is for you. The Back to Basics discipline program gets results and its effects could be life changing.

The purpose of discipline is to teach children certain behaviors are appropriate and others are not. However, there is much more to it than the short-term goal of teaching children right and wrong behaviors. There are long-term goals for our children to live good lives, be good people and do good things. Responsibility, respect, self-control, honesty and compassion are the fundamental character traits which lead to living good lives, being good people and doing good things. They are the long-term goals of discipline, and I assure you they're not difficult to achieve. My husband and I chose this discipline program for our children because we knew discipline in accordance with specific rules was the most effective way to achieve our objectives.

This book provides many stories and examples to show you how Back to Basics works. You will see for each disciplinary event, there is a specific lesson learned directly related to the development of character. Back to Basics is not a new idea. I was raised this way, and I raised my children this way. I'll bet our grandmothers and their mothers before them would recognize many features of this discipline program. Through this program your children will learn the virtues of patience, understanding, kindness and consideration. *They* will be well-behaved children, good students, trustworthy teenagers and grow up to be extraordinary adults. Their capacity to enjoy life to the fullest and achieve success will be greatly enhanced.

Back to Basics discipline is founded on a single principle: disciplined children are happier children. Simply put, children have two primary needs—to feel safe and loved. Children acquire their feelings of security from parents who establish and enforce boundaries with absolute consistency, thereby creating a predictable environment. We all know children feel loved when parents are generous with affection and praise. Security and love are two sides of the same coin—*equal amounts of love and discipline*. When they are in balance, so is the child. Since their primary needs are satisfied, disciplined children are happier children.

Have you ever noticed how undisciplined children seem to be so unhappy? They're angry, aggressive, contrary and unruly. Look around and you will see many children whose parents are forthcoming with the *love* part of the equation and a little too light on the discipline side. With love and discipline out of balance, so are the children. For many of them the natural sweetness inside is suppressed and will not bloom until their primary needs are met.

Back to Basics is a complete program which provides children with equal amounts of love and discipline. It includes seven essential elements. The first element is *High Standards*. It's about deciding how you want your children to turn out. If you're like me, you want your children to do what they are told without whining and complaining, to know the difference between right and wrong and to tell the truth. In short, you want them to have good character, which means holding them to High Standards.

The second essential element is *Effective Method*, which means using the most Effective Method of discipline. Yes, spanking (or paddling) is part of Back to Basics discipline. Let me make absolutely clear abusing children is not what this discipline program is about. When I use the term *spanking*, I mean no more than a few swats on the bottom with your hand. In fact, I will demonstrate how a few swats on the behind is a loving and effective way to discipline and spanking is *not* a last resort and *not* an act of anger.

I understand your impulse to cringe at the very mention of the word *spanking*, so I'll be gentle with you by using *swat* or *paddle* now and then. I promise to help you understand a firm hand applied at the right age, for the right reason, means never losing your cool and never getting to the point of having to scream at, denigrate or physically abuse a child.

I will also demonstrate you need not choose between the timeout and the spanking—there are indeed benefits derived from both methods. The trick is to know which method is more suitable in each disciplinary situation.

Seven Golden Rules, the third essential element, are the backbone of the discipline program. These rules will ensure you will be teaching lessons, earning respect and becoming the effective parent you should be.

The fourth essential element, *Absolute No-Nos*, is about disciplining kids for the right reasons. This is where those important character traits come in to play.

There are five behaviors in children which are just not acceptable. I call them the Absolute No-Nos.

The fifth essential element, *Separate Worlds*, is about keeping the "kid world" and the "adult world" separate. Some things should be off limits to children in order to preserve the innocence of childhood and maintain a proper parent-child relationship.

The sixth essential element is *Sibling Relationships*. Sibling relationships are both complicated and wonderful. It's important for parents to realize things they do can either destroy or nurture Sibling Relationships.

Home Environment, the seventh essential element, is about things parents should do to create warm, loving, safe and happy Home Environments for children.

This discipline program is based on my mother's rules for discipline. Fortunately, she knew the wisdom of teaching me how to discipline my children. She was a wise and generous mentor, for which I am truly grateful. I followed my mother's advice and stuck to her rules for discipline to the letter. The result: the best kids you can imagine!

It is now my duty to teach my children about discipline so my mother's legacy of raising extraordinary children continues. My original intention was to create a written list of the rules of discipline. However, once I got started, I began to realize there was so much more than a simple list of rules. Memories of how I was raised began to bubble up. Delightful family stories began to pour from my brain as if the floodgates had been opened. It became apparent my memories and family stories helped to convey the purpose of each rule which is more clearly understood in the context of application. What started out to be a simple list of rules is now this book.

In the following chapters I provide specific examples of what to do in certain situations. However, it would be impossible to address every scenario which might come up. The idea is to give you the fundamentals of Back to Basics so you can draw upon them when disciplining your children.

Keep in mind a crucial element of any discipline program is parental judgment. It's important to remember each child is unique and each child's discipline requirements are unique. The rule of thumb is to use the least amount of punishment required to get results. Some kids need stern warnings, some need just one swat on the bottom and others need good paddlings. You know your child better than anyone, and you must rely on your judgment when applying discipline.

You'll get the most out of this book by first reading it from cover to cover. Then, occasionally, you will want to review Chapters Four and Five to keep the Rules and the No-nos uppermost in your mind. (After reading Chapters Four and Five you'll know what I mean.) Finally, you'll want to keep this book in a handy place for quick, easy reference. This is the key to raising the best kids you can imagine.

1

Back to Basics
Discipline in Action

"In my mother's house,
kids felt loved and welcome. . ."

My Mother's House

Before I presume to tell you how to raise your children, let me give you some insight into my upbringing, which is a great example of Back to Basics in action.

My parents were married in 1945 during World War II. My mother was only sixteen and my father only seventeen. This year they will celebrate their 58th wedding anniversary.

I am extremely proud of my father, a World War II Veteran who served four years during the war. Like many people of their generation, they settled down after the war to the business of having babies. Hence, my brothers and I are part of the generation often referred to as baby boomers. I am the youngest of three and have two older brothers. Mitch is two years older than me, and Dick is two years older than Mitch.

Mom and Dad were quite a partnership. Mom was a full-time housewife and mother. She was so good at it that I am always telling her, had she been a career woman, she would have been running the company in just a matter of a few years. She was an efficiency expert. Every day of every week was planned. For example, Monday was laundry day. Throughout my childhood, if the washing machine was running, it was Monday.

More important, we were spanked when we needed it at a very young age and learned to respect and fear Mom in a healthy way. In our house we were not allowed to sass or talk back. We did what we were told—the first time. If we had to be told a second time, the consequence was a spanking. We were not beaten or abused, we were not humiliated, nor was our self-esteem destroyed. We were taught to be accountable for our actions, not to lie and to respect all authority figures, including our parents, our friends' parents and our teachers. Most of the time, Mom only needed to give a certain look, or snap her fingers, and we understood she was not happy about something we were doing. There was no yelling, nagging and screaming in our house.

When our family visited friends' homes, my brothers and I played outside. If it was raining or nighttime, we could play in the house but were not allowed to run through the house. Even when the children who lived in the home were allowed to run through the house, we were not. If my mother thought things were getting out of hand, she would have us sit on the floor next to her until it was time to go. She once told me she never wanted anyone to dread having us over for a visit. Mom would take it personally if somebody was less than pleased to see her children. Looking back, I am appreciative of the fact she made sure we were liked.

I was treated with kindness and genuine affection by other adults—the kind of affection you give a child you are truly happy to see.

After I was grown, Mom and I had many discussions about the way I was raised and she explained her reasons for the way she did things. It made so much sense to me. I am lucky her responsibility as a parent didn't end with food, shelter and education. It was much more. Mom wasn't a member of the PTA and didn't belong to a car pool. She never volunteered in the classroom and she didn't spend half the day driving us to after school activities. She probably wouldn't be described as a super-mom by today's standards because she didn't do those things. But in my book, she was the real thing. She was a mom where it counted. Her High Standards and persistence in discipline were the greatest gifts of all.

Growing up as one of Del and Jean Campbell's kids wasn't all serious business and spankings. In fact, since spanking was so effective, there was actually a lot less disciplining going on in the house, which left more time for being a family. My parents never fought or argued in front of us kids and we weren't allowed to bicker and fight with each other. Mom didn't believe in arguing, she despised the very thought of it. She said arguing never accomplished anything and was a waste of time. Therefore, there was no arguing in the Campbell house. Since we didn't waste time challenging Mom's authority or fighting, our family life was peaceful and pleasant.

In my mother's house, kids felt loved and welcome. My friends, and my brothers' friends, liked coming over to our house. They enjoyed the loving, peaceful environment. They would come to our house after school rather than go home and fight with their parents. I had cousins who knew they had to be good at my house. My mother was known as mean Aunt Jean. It's funny how they thought she was mean, but they loved coming over. It was a place where they were required to behave and they liked it. Doesn't this say a lot about how kids want to be made to behave?

My brothers and I did not go through rebellious phases like so many teenagers do. We were teenagers in the sixties, when teenage rebellion was just beginning to be the phenomenon of the century. I think the entire baby boomer generation rebelled. It was the hippy decade, replete with sex, drugs and irresponsible behavior. Everyone was "looking for themselves" and living by the motto "if it feels good, do it." My brothers and I were not lured by all of that nonsense. We knew who we were, and we were definitely not rebellious or irresponsible. Peer pressure wasn't a problem for us because we didn't need to feel like we belonged to something other than our own family. We didn't feel we needed anybody's approval. We had plenty of self-esteem, which I believe is the best defense against peer pressure. I think we all lost friends at one time or another to drugs. I hung around with a group of girls in my neighborhood when I was about thirteen. We had slumber parties, rode horses, went to the movies and went ice-skating. We did many fun things together. Once we got into high school, we all went our separate ways. One of those friends, Debbie, died from a drug overdose when she was just seventeen. She had gone to a party where people were doing drugs and her body was found the next morning on the front lawn.

My mother told me something when I was a young teenager just starting to enjoy some freedom. What she told me stayed with me all my life. She said, "I can't be with you twenty-four hours a day, seven days a week. In case you are ever in a situation where you might be tempted to do something you shouldn't be doing, ask yourself , *what would my mother say if she were watching me right now?*" She added, "If you can't come home and happily tell me everything you did while you were out with your friends, you have been doing some things you shouldn't be doing." I took this to heart. I always wanted Mom and Dad to be proud of me. That's why you would not ever have seen me at a party like the one Debbie went to the night she died. I had sense enough to not put myself in a situation where someone would even approach me with drugs.

I was a newlywed living in Panama (my husband was in the Navy at the time) when I got the news about Debbie. Mom sent me the local newspaper article. Enclosed with the clipping was a letter from Mom saying she was thankful she didn't have to worry about me and the choices I made in my life. I immediately sat down, wrote her back and set her straight. . . I let her know I am the person I am because of her and she only needs to thank herself.

When I was a child, I was not allowed to be rude or selfish. Most things we were corrected for were directly related to character traits. We were required to be respectful, quiet, obedient and polite. There were plenty of house rules like no running in the house, cleaning up after yourself and making sure you came home when Mom told you to be home. It was not too much to ask of a kid.

When we became teenagers, Mom was more lenient. She didn't need to get after us for being rude or disrespectful—we were actually great kids. We enjoyed more freedom than our friends did. Mom was generous because she trusted us. She told us, until we did something to take her trust away, we had it completely. She'd say, "God help you if you lose my trust. It will only take one mistake and you will never have it again. I will never be able to trust you, and you will lose your freedom." I was so lucky! At sixteen I was allowed to get my driver's license and had lots of freedom to use it. I was mindful of not doing anything to jeopardize my mother's trust. She gave me the power, it was all up to me. If I wanted to continue to enjoy her trust and the total freedom which came with it, I would stay out of trouble—and I did.

Mom would get after us for not doing what we were told, talking back, lying or having a bad attitude. But she was easy in a lot of other ways. We were always able to sleep in without guilt on Saturdays. Our rooms didn't have to be neat and tidy all of the time. If we let our rooms get so bad you couldn't walk in them, she would make us clean them up but she didn't have a cow every time we dropped a sock on the floor and didn't pick it up. I had friends whose mothers would allow them to be extremely disrespectful. Their mothers would tell them to do things and they would tell them *no*, or that they would do it later (which meant it would never get done). You can imagine my shock when I would see my friends getting away with such behavior. Those same mothers would throw the biggest fit over a messy room. I had a friend whose mother called her and made her go home to pick up a pair of gloves she'd left on top of her dresser. My mother's response was, as a parent, you have to pick the right things to get upset about. She never thought a messy room threatened our character. She believed doing what you were told, attitude and honesty were more important. My mom wasn't a nag. I didn't dread coming home because she was going to be on my case about something.

I was never grounded. Being grounded was a punishment all of my friends suffered for being bad. It seemed like somebody was always grounded. I didn't even know what being grounded was; I had to ask my friend what it was when she told me she couldn't come over because she was grounded. She was probably grounded for talking back or not cleaning her room. My mother never believed in grounding as a means of punishment. She thought grounding your kids was something you did because you failed to discipline them when they were younger. If you did the job right from the beginning, grounding wasn't necessary.

When we were teenagers Mom and Dad talked to us like we were adults. They treated us with respect. They gave us responsibility and independence appropriate for our ages and we rose to the occasion each and every time. We loved being treated like we had brains and we responded accordingly. If we had been spoiled, selfish teenagers like so many others were, that's exactly how they would have treated us. But we were not spoiled, selfish teenagers. We were mature and responsible. Family time was especially enjoyable and rewarding during our teen years. This is exactly the opposite of what most people say about their teenage years. I have to add, this was during the sixties!

Now, you probably know more about me than you think necessary. But consider the healthy things about my mother's house—daily routine, house rules which were respected, children who never talked back, a Home Environment free from nagging, arguing and fighting, a place where kids felt loved and welcome, and respectful, trustworthy teenagers.

My husband and I used the same methods my mother used and, as a result, my children enjoyed the same happy Home Environment. With this kind of success for two generations, I'd be crazy not to pass this legacy on to my children. Additionally, I feel compelled to share my success with all who are interested.

I've taken my mother's teachings, packaged them together with childhood memories and personal successes in raising my own children and named it "Back to Basics Discipline." It's not a new or untested concept, it's merely getting back to what was once a way of life.

2

High Standards

"It all starts with holding kids to
higher standards of behavior . . ."

The First Essential Element
in Back to Basics Discipline

Raising children is, without a doubt, the most important job there is. Whether you work or stay at home, nothing you do will ever be as important as raising your children. It is a career; it's important and should be taken seriously. If you gave up college or a great job to stay home and raise children, you have not given up something more important for something less important. What could be more important than raising happy, healthy children?

Having said that, it seems logical there should be careful consideration about how you want your children to turn out. What qualities do you want them to have? What qualities will your children need in order for them to be able to go out into this big world and achieve happiness and success? I believe you should set your sights high and success is completely dependent upon discipline.

The Epidemic of Unruly Children

Undisciplined children are prevalent in America today, and it's a disgrace. Our schools are filled with them leaving teachers with the daunting task of trying to educate children who have no respect for rules or authority. You can't go outside of your home without seeing one or two situations where children are acting out. They seem to be crying, "I need some boundaries! I need somebody who loves me enough to set limits! I need someone to look up to and respect! I need someone who makes me feel safe by always enforcing the law—someone I can count on!"

Recently, I observed two instances involving the behavior of children which illustrates what we all witness on a regular basis. The tragedy is nobody seems to think there is anything wrong with the way those children are behaving.

This first story is about a woman in the grocery store who was in the checkout line in front of my husband and me. Her son appeared to be about six years old and his name was Michael. He was fidgeting around the shopping cart, reaching in to touch everything and trying to climb in. His little hands were as busy as they could be. There was something inside the shopping cart he decided he wanted to get hold of, and it was clear his mother didn't want him to have it. As she was putting items from the cart onto the conveyor belt to be checked out, she kept repeating things like, "Michael no, leave that alone." After the basket was emptied, Michael looked around to see what else he could get into. He spotted the candy rack, and the hubbub continued. He picked up a bag of candy and went over to his mom who was waiting to see what her purchase total was. Several times she told him to put the candy back and reminded him there was a bowl of candy at home. He never let up on her. He kept whining and begging for her to buy the candy.

Finally, she started to pay her bill and it looked like they were ready to leave. Upon realizing he had lost the battle for the candy, he relented and put the candy back on the rack. Although he knew she'd already paid for the groceries and he had been too late with the candy, clever little Michael vied for his mother's praise for putting the candy back. His mom was so relieved it was over she told him what a good boy he was. I wondered if she realized how she was duped into telling him he was good, especially when he was anything but good the whole time they were in line!

The next story is about a little boy in a department store. He looked like he was about five years old and his name was Mathew. My husband and I noticed him and his mother in the store aisle while waiting for some assistance from a store clerk. The mother caught my attention when she grabbed her son's arm and said to him sharply, "Do you want a timeout?" It was apparent she was at the end of her rope. It was equally apparent Mathew wasn't the least bit afraid of the timeout. There could be two possible reasons for why she didn't elicit fear in Mathew when she threatened him with a timeout. One, timeouts only work when removal from a fun activity is involved. Two, she probably never followed through with her threats.

A few minutes later we got in line and, sure enough, Mathew and his mother were just in front of us. He continued to leave his mother's side to touch everything he could get his hands on. She had a stroller to keep her place in line while she ran after her son, which happened three or four times. When they got up to the counter she reached into her purse to find her wallet and he took off again. The wallet tumbled to the floor and she chased after him. This time she wedged him between her body and the counter pushing against his body with hers so he couldn't get away. It was a struggle for her to get her wallet and pay the clerk. But that wasn't the end of it. When she backed up to release him, he grabbed the handle of the stroller, looked at her and said, "I want to push it." The emphasis was on *I*, and he said it with defiance. By that time she was tired of fighting. She relinquished the stroller to him and out the door they went. Everyone in the store was glad they were finally gone.

The poor little kid! He needed somebody to teach him to be still and mind. What his mother didn't realize was, he was perfectly capable of being still and minding, but she never made him do it. Consequently, a trip to the department store was absolutely exhausting and it didn't need to be that way. When I see those situations, I don't understand why mothers put up with it. I could tell by her son's demeanor the only form of punishment used on him was the timeout, or the threat of a timeout, and it wasn't working. He had ignored every command to stop touching things in the store.

I have two comments about those stories. First, if the mothers had begun teaching their sons to mind *before* they were two years old, the moms and kids would be happier and trips to the store would be much less stressful. Second, it's a little late, but not too late. The mothers should be a little less tolerant. They need to raise their standards for how they expect their sons to behave. I have no doubt if they did, the boys would respond in very positive ways.

What's in Your Future?

Fast-forward and imagine your child is 16 years old. What type of individual do you hope he or she is? Imagine your teenager coming home from school, walking through the front door and encountering you in the entryway. What will the exchange between the two of you be like? Will he or she avoid eye contact with you, run up the stairs, slam the door and say, "Leave me alone," when you ask how their day went? Or, will he or she come through the door, make eye contact with you and smile? Will the two of you chat for a few minutes about their day? Will your child have a conversation with you and not leave the room until it's over?

Consider the difference in the two examples. The first teenager will not have any respect for you, and will probably have low self-esteem. He will lack emotional maturity and be more concerned about avoiding contact with you than anything else. You and your feelings will not matter to him. This child will be selfish, rude and hostile. The second teen will be well adjusted and happy. He will have nothing to hide from you and will be happy to stay and discuss his day with you. The second 16-year-old will be mature and confident.

Is a rebellious teenager in your future? If you have an undisciplined child today, you will likely be looking at a rebellious teenager in a few years. Rebellious teenagers control the house. They have no respect for their parents who, undoubtedly, relinquished control many years earlier.

Typical characteristics of such teens are hostility, anger, disobedience and disrespect. Because they lack self-control, they are vulnerable to drug and alcohol abuse, sexual promiscuity and are especially vulnerable to peer pressure. Some decisions they make during their teen years can be very costly and self-destructive. They are prone to making stupid mistakes they will pay for the rest of their lives. They are frustrated because they want to be treated like adults and enjoy adult privileges. However, their parents can't treat them like adults because they still behave like spoiled children. The truth is, they are still yearning for someone to enforce boundaries. Any attempts to discipline them will be futile, and any helpful advice offered to them will be acrimoniously rejected. Not surprisingly, they purposely make decisions which will cause pain, especially for their parents. Their parents, who think they are providing them with everything, wonder why they are rewarded with one of life's greatest heartaches: an ungrateful child. All they can do at this point is hope they straighten out by the time they are adults.

Shouldn't We Expect More?

Over the past 30 years or so a gradual decline in standards for behavior in children has occurred. Media influence and popular trends, creating pressure on all of us, have crept into the home and changed how parents raise their kids. Many mothers and fathers today are so meek and hesitant about disciplining their children, they seem to have abdicated their most important responsibility. Predominant ideas about disciplining children today may be popular and widely used, but are not necessarily the right way to go.

Has America lost faith in its children? Are we lowering the standards for behavior, academic achievement and morality because we no longer believe our children are capable of greatness? Consider the hypocrisy of society today. Everyone seems to be extremely concerned about the well-being of children and everything is about them. Politicians love to use the phrase "for the children" for their own self-serving purposes. All that hype, yet we think so little of them as to believe children are not capable of good behavior.

One of my pet peeves is the way children are portrayed on television shows. Nearly all children are represented as spoiled, disrespectful brats on television, which makes bad behavior in our off-screen children more acceptable and normal. That way, we can all feel like we're doing a good job raising our children. However, aren't we letting our children down by not expecting more?

The sad truth is appalling behavior in children has become the norm. It's okay if children throw tantrums—after all they're just expressing themselves. It has become common belief it's okay if children behave like wild monkeys in public, talk back to their parents and teachers and it's okay if they are rude. I flatly disagree. It's not okay to permit kids to do those things. I don't believe our children's best interests are served, or those of society in general, by being so permissive.

Imagine the Possibilities

I have old-fashioned ideas about how children should act. Like my mother, I knew exactly what I expected of my children. I wanted them to do what they were told without complaining or talking back. I wanted them to know the difference between right and wrong. I wanted them to mind the teacher and do their homework. I wanted them to always tell me the truth. But I was also looking a few years down the road. I refused to believe dealing with a rebellious teenager was in my future. My ultimate goal was to prepare them for adulthood. I simply wanted them to have the best possible shot at achieving success and happiness.

Imagine the possibilities. Everyone enjoys disciplined children. They're courteous and respectful, they know how to sit still and be quiet. Those children are a teacher's dream! They do well in school because they do not feel the need to constantly challenge the teacher's authority or compete for attention. Instead, they listen and learn. Disciplined children are intrinsically kind, considerate, sweet and so easy to love. Those children excel at life for an abundance of reasons including sound moral and ethical backgrounds, the ability to control their emotions and compassion for others. They have an inner strength upon which they draw when faced with life's difficult challenges. They know right from wrong. As adults, they succeed in their personal and professional lives. There is nothing more rewarding for a parent.

Actions Speak Louder Than Words

It's easy to say you want good children, that your standards are high, but the key to actually achieving those standards is much more in what you do than what you say. Tolerating bad behavior is a roadblock to achieving High Standards.

One big misconception about raising children today is the notion tolerance equals good parenting. In fact, by being permissive and tolerant you are cheating your child out of the chance to learn valuable lessons which lead to development of strong character.

Don't confuse tolerance with patience. Patience is indeed a virtue. A parent who spends countless hours teaching a child to ride a bicycle is a patient parent. But a parent who tolerates bad behavior is foolish. Let me explain.

Imagine your toddler throwing a temper tantrum because you say she cannot go outside and play until she finishes her macaroni and cheese. A tolerant parent might justify the child's behavior by saying something like:

"It isn't that important. I'll let it go."

"It probably is important, but I'll let it go just this once."

"It's a phase—she'll grow out of it"

There are many reasons people fall into this trap. They are too busy, too tired or simply too lazy to get up out of their chairs and discipline a child who desperately needs it. Now here's the part about being foolish. It *is* important, you should *never* let it go just this once and she *won't* grow out of it. The little behavior problems tolerated today will become monumental behavior problems tomorrow. For a glimpse of those monumental behavior problems of tomorrow, refer back a couple of paragraphs to my description of the typical rebellious teenager.

Specific behaviors which should not be tolerated, including temper tantrums, are covered in Chapter Five. The point is to realize having High Standards is articulated through both your *verbal commitment* and your *physical actions*.

Yes, We Should Expect More

Children are capable of being well behaved, being quiet and polite, being good in school and of being taught to mind without complaining or whining. Children are not only *capable*, but *deserve* the opportunity to be extraordinary. Give your children the tools they need to have the greatest chance at success and happiness. Teach them responsibility, respect, self-control, honesty and compassion. Decide that anything less is just not good enough. Don't tolerate bad behavior. Expect and insist on good behavior.

It all starts with holding kids to High Standards— the first essential element in Back to Basics discipline.

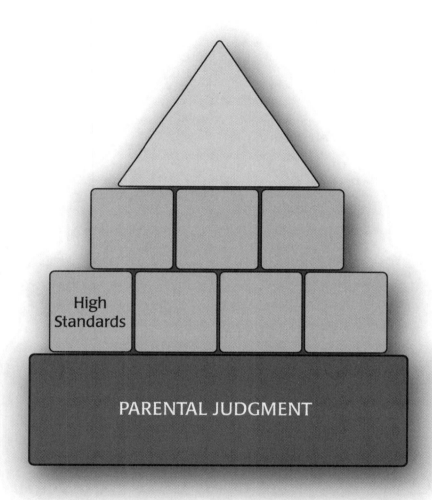

3

Effective Method

*"People mistakenly believe
they must choose between the
timeout and the spanking."*

The Second Essential Element
in Back to Basics Discipline

So far we've covered how important it is to discipline children and how High Standards for behavior are key to turning out spectacular kids. Many people would agree with me up to this point. However, using the most Effective Method of discipline is where I take off on a different direction than the current trend. As you may know, the current trend in discipline is very hands-off, with the timeout being the most widely used form of punishment. Most people believe they must choose between the timeout and the spanking.

I don't believe it's a matter of choosing between spankings and timeouts. I believe it's a matter of bringing back spanking in order to fill a need the timeout may not be fulfilling—instilling respect in children. Since the phasing out of spanking in recent years, more parents today don't seem to be able to control their children. The majority of children today are displaying an obvious lack of respect for their parents' authority.

The success of any discipline program depends on being able to control your child, which is directly related to his or her respect for your authority. Spanking is going to be your best tool for teaching your child to respect your authority. This important lesson must be taught at an early age before it becomes a problem (see Chapter Four). The timeout, on the other hand, is an appropriate form of punishment for a child who has already learned to respect your authority.

I remember sitting for a timeout when I was six (before there was actually a word for it). One Sunday, my father took the whole family to a nearby recreational lake for a day of swimming and picnicking with friends. There was a certain beach area roped off and the children were all told to stay within that area. For some reason I strayed into an area I was not supposed to be in and it didn't take my mother long to notice. She calmly walked over to me, took my hand, walked me up to the blanket on the beach and took off my life jacket. I was not allowed to play in the water for the rest of the day. This was torture for me, and I *did* learn my lesson.

A common mistake today is to misuse the timeout, as demonstrated by Mathew's mother in the previous chapter. When she screamed at him, "Do you want a timeout?" I was left wondering, "A timeout from *what*?" From walking around in a department store? Not exactly a big deal in Mathew's world. But, lets say they were in the park and Mathew was having fun playing with other children and did something he wasn't supposed to do, like put sand in his little brother's hair. In this case, a timeout would be appropriate because Mathew would be removed from an activity he was enjoying.

The bottom line is the timeout should involve removing a child from an enjoyable activity. Sitting a child in a room or a corner for a few minutes of quiet time may send him the message that sitting still and being quiet is punishment. I believe a child's ability to sit still and be quiet is a virtue. After all, children should be expected to sit still and be quiet at the dinner table, in school and in church without thinking they are being punished.

The following story illustrates popular misconceptions about spanking. It also supports my opinion the timeout by itself is falling short of teaching children respect. On a recent television talk show, the entire episode was dedicated to the belief spanking is unacceptable and should be eliminated. The host emphatically stated it was abuse, without any dialogue about exactly what spanking is. Without any clarification as to the definition of spanking, it entirely invalidated the integrity of the topic. When, in reality, some people still believe spanking is just a few swats on the bottom—not everyone believes spanking is child abuse.

Guests on this particular talk show were women who were extremely distressed because they couldn't control their children. The timeout was the disciplinary method of choice for most of them. In my opinion, the show failed to make a case for the timeout in lieu of spanking. Film clips were shown of their kids, all between the ages of about five and eight, in the midst of the most horrible behavior. They were throwing temper tantrums, whining and being defiant. One of the clips showed a girl of about seven whose mother told her she could not go outside to play because she didn't finish a meal, or some such reason. The little girl told her mother *no,* and proceeded to put her shoes on and go outside. The next scene showed the mother strong-arming the little girl back into the house. It was more violent and abusive than a few swats on the behind a few years earlier would have been.

The discussion centered on the mothers and what they should do about their stress. Not one word was spoken about the lack of respect for authority apparent in their children.

Two of the mothers on the show claimed they tried spanking, but it didn't work. After hearing more of the discussion, it turned out those mothers had waited until they were angry before taking action—big mistake. What they needed was more information about spanking. Specifically, if anyone is going to spank their children, they need to follow certain rules (see Chapter Four). Inconsistency in discipline or spanking for the wrong reasons will get very poor results.

Everyone, including the so-called "expert" on the show, missed the point. If the guest mothers had instilled respect in their children before they were five years old, they wouldn't be faced with such unmanageable children today.

The Cop-Outs

There are a lot of excuses for not spanking. The most popular excuse is equating spanking with abuse, as was done on the television talk show. Spanking is no more than a few swats on the bottom and, when used following the Seven Golden Rules, is the most effective way to discipline children. It is the furthest thing from abuse. You spank your child because you love him or her and you want to teach important lessons.

Another popular misconception is the belief spanking teaches violence. This is an unfair statement which implies spanking is a violent, knee-jerk reaction by an angry parent. You will find, after reading the following chapters, spanking should only consist of a few swats on the bottom, should only be done by a calm, controlled parent who is not angry and should be done for the right reasons. By making sure you are not angry when you punish, your child will know the punishment was because of his actions and not because of your anger. Therein lies the difference.

Violent behavior in children has more to do with the parent's state of mind during the act of spanking and the overall consistency of discipline a child receives. I encourage you to look around at children you know and observe their behavior. There are children who are happy and play well with other children, and there are children who seem very unhappy, aggressive and sometimes violent with other children. Parents of the happy, nonviolent children typically use spanking to teach respect for their authority, never spank when they are angry, are consistent in the application of discipline and they started discipline before the child was two years old. Basically, the children's primary needs of feeling safe and loved have been satisfied as evidenced by their sweet dispositions.

Parents of aggressive children typically don't believe in spanking (and if they do, they only spank when they are angry), are not consistent with discipline and did not teach their children respect for authority at a young age. Those children's primary needs have not been satisfied, which is often manifested through aggressive behavior.

Many people won't spank their children because

they are afraid their children won't love them if they do. Nonsense! If you think this way, you are missing the point. Your child doesn't need you for a friend or buddy. Your child needs you to be a parent. People who use this excuse are focusing on their own self-serving fears rather than the needs of their children.

The following is a great story about my mother which illustrates where her focus was. When my brothers and I were very young, we were at a family gathering at my grandmother's house. All my aunts and uncles and cousins were there. It was a nice summer day and my mother made my brothers and me stay outside to play. My cousins were allowed to run in and out of the house, which always drove my mom crazy. When it came time to eat dinner, my mother called us in and had us sit on the floor along one wall in the family room out of the way of all of the chaos. She said she would fix our plates and we could take them outside to eat. We sat there with our legs crossed, patiently waiting for our dinners. My cousins, on the other hand, were in the middle of things, getting in the way and creating even more chaos. When one of my aunts noticed Dick, Mitch, and me sitting there on the floor she remarked, "Jean, you're so mean. Your kids aren't going to love you when they grow up." Mom's quick retort was, "I don't want them to love me—I want them to mind me." I wasn't close enough to hear all of this, but Mom told me about it when I was older. I laughed when she told me what she'd said. I could just imagine the look of horror on my aunt's face. The truth is my mother knew she had nothing to worry about as far as us loving her. Her priority was doing what was best for us. She knew, in addition to being adored, disciplined children developed the character traits which allowed them to live more satisfying and productive lives.

Mom knew it all started with discipline, and then all of the good things—obedience, respect and love—would naturally follow. She was right.

Spanking Q and A

So what exactly is spanking? In this book, spanking means no more than five swats on the bottom or thigh with your hand. You never punch a child, you never slap a child's face or hit their head. Just swat, but make sure it is felt enough to be a deterrent. It will have no effect if the child doesn't feel it. Feeling pain is how Nature teaches all living things important lessons. When we touch fire, it hurts. Right? Therefore, we are not likely to touch fire again—ever. Your swat must be firm enough to teach a lesson. A one-year-old needs only one swat, maybe two depending on the circumstance and degree of defiance being displayed. As your child gets older, he or she may need up to five good swats.

Are there rules for spanking? Yes. I call them the Seven Golden Rules and they are described in detail in Chapter Four. Adherence to the rules will ensure every spanking is an important lesson learned and *not* an act of anger.

Where should you spank? As with any form of punishment, it should always be done in private. Never spank a child in the presence of others, which would result in humiliating and embarrassing the child. This brings to mind the popular question of what to do about disciplining a child in public. You should never spank a child in public. My theory is if you teach children *no* means no at home, it will carry over to when you're in

35

the grocery store. Some will figure out you will not discipline them in public and try to take advantage of the situation. By the time they figure this out, they are old enough to handle with a little warning.

For example, the first time your toddler discovers he can throw a fit in the store if he doesn't get his way, whisper in a stern tone something like, "You be a good boy in the store!" When you get out to the car, remind him he was not a good boy in the store. The next time you go to the grocery store, before you leave the house, issue the same warning, "You be a good boy in the store!"

I went through this with my children and my warnings usually worked because I was so consistent with discipline at home. However, one time I had to warn the misbehaving child of the spanking he would receive when we got home. I followed through with the spanking—and that worked. The problem never recurred. Remember, your child must be old enough to understand the concept of the threat and remember why he is getting the spanking after a period of time has passed. If a child is younger than two years old, he may not understand. Every child is different but I believe parents know when their children are capable of understanding, "You're getting a spanking when we get home for being bad in the store."

What age should you begin to spank? Spanking is the best way to teach children respect, which is more effectively done between the ages of one and five. If you do this right, there will be very few spankings after the age of five. However, I do not advocate a full spanking for a one-year-old child, only one or two swats.

What are the reasons you should spank? There are specific behaviors which affect the development of good character in children and warrant good paddlings. I call them the *Absolute No-Nos* and they are discussed at length in Chapter Five.

When is it too late to begin spanking if the timeout hasn't worked? If you are one of the unfortunate parents misled by all of the "experts" into thinking the timeout alone would do the job and now find yourself with a child who needs to be disciplined, it's not too late to begin. If your child is younger than twelve years old and generally undisciplined, it will be more frustrating and take longer if you start a discipline program now, but something must be done. I believe children crave discipline and would still benefit from it, however late coming it is.

One Spanking is Worth a Thousand Timeouts

In short, there is room for both the timeout and the spanking in a disciplinary program. The timeout can be a useful addition to the discipline program if used correctly, but not until the important lessons about respect are learned.

Whatever you call it, spanking, paddling, or a few firm swats on the behind, it will make a more lasting impression on your child than any other form of discipline. It will get his attention and teach him to respect you. In the long run you will find, because you have taught your child to respect your authority, you will have little need for the timeout. A few swats in the beginning will save you hours and hours of timeouts and counting to three later on.

Using the most Effective Method of discipline is the second essential element in Back to Basics discipline.

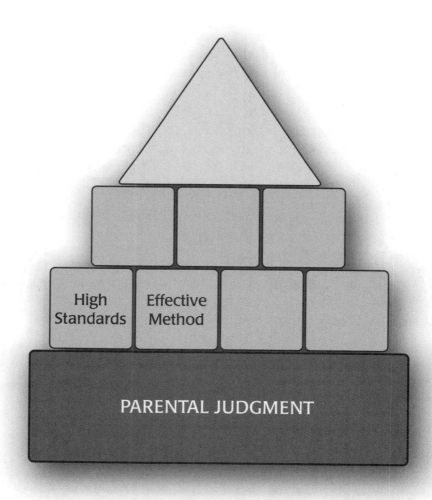

4

Seven Golden Rules

*" . . .you will be teaching the lessons,
earning the respect and becoming the
effective parent you should be."*

The Third Essential Element
in Back to Basics Discipline

So far, we've discussed High Standards of behavior
and using the most Effective Method of discipline—
both crucially important elements in Back to Basics
discipline. Now I'll let you in on the real nitty gritty of
discipline: the Seven Golden Rules.

1. Start early

2. Be consistent

3. Don't delay

4. Never punish when you're angry

5. Always follow through with a threat

6. Never apologize, explain or negotiate

7. Maintain a united front

Rule One—Start Early

Many parents wait until their children are in their

teens, then decide it's time to start clamping down. Suddenly it becomes important to enforce boundaries. Now that driving cars, girlfriends or boyfriends and parties are in the picture, the same parents who were very permissive when their children were young are now determined to get tough. The outcome is very predictable but the order is completely backward.

The secret is to be tough on kids when they are very young. It is possible and, in fact much easier, to plant the seeds of responsibility, respect, self-control, honesty and compassion at an early age. Amazingly, you will be able to lighten up when your children are teenagers. As they become older, you will gradually begin to trust them and give them more responsibility and more freedom. Because you are easing up on them, rather than clamping down at a time when they naturally want to have more independence, everyone is happier. They get to do stuff and you get to sleep at night, knowing your teenager has enough sense to make the right decisions.

The following two stories further illustrate the point of starting early.

When our kids were growing up we lived in a home surrounded by an acre of walnut trees. It was a rural area in a small town, and there were no sidewalks on our street which ended in a cul-de-sac. It was a quiet neighborhood with very little traffic to worry about, which made it a great place for kids to play outdoors. A shallow streambed cut across the front of our property. It had a clean, sandy bottom and served as an oversized sand box the kids loved to play in. Water flowed in it only when it rained, and sometimes for a few days afterwards.

In the fall of 1983 it had rained more than usual and the stream flowed for a few days before drying up. One morning, my mother and I were in the front yard and my two youngest daughters, Janette, age five, and April, not quite three years old, were playing in the streambed. Mom and I heard a strange sound at the same time and looked at each other. As it got louder, I looked upstream and saw a three-foot wall of water rushing toward the girls playing in the streambed. In a calm but serious voice I said, "Janette, April, come here now!" They both immediately stopped what they were doing and scampered up to me completely unaware of the approaching danger. In a flash the water went rushing past. Mom and I looked at each other in shock. If the girls had hesitated at all to come when I called them, they would have been swept away. It would have killed them both. I found out later a contractor working on a housing project upstream had used his tractor to dam up the water a few days before and had chosen that particular morning to level it and let the water go.

Fortunately, I began teaching my children at an early age they must obey me without question. It was not necessary for me to negotiate and plead with them to come out of the streambed. Can you honestly think of many children you know who would actually come out of the streambed on the first command? Imagine what would have happened if I'd had to take up valuable time telling them over and over to come out, or if I'd had to threaten them with a timeout on the count of three.

This next story, told to me by my mother who was an eyewitness, is about a little boy who wasn't so lucky as Janette and April. His name was Jackie and he was two or three years old at the time. My mother was about five years old and she and her mother were at Jackie's house visiting. The house had an old open-flame heater sitting on the floor. It had ornate cast iron down the sides and across the top. My mother vividly recalls Jackie's mother leaving the room, and as she did she turned back and pointed her finger at the heater and said to Jackie, "No, no!" She had no sooner left the room than he deliberately went right over to the heater and reached his hand out to touch it. Because it was hot he jerked his hand back quickly. In the process, his hand caught the ironwork on top and the heater came down upon him. His clothes instantly caught fire. His mother rushed in and put the fire out, but not until he had suffered third degree burns. His legs and body were scarred for life, not to mention the pain and trauma he suffered from the burns.

Within every household there must be a hierarchy of power. Parents on top, kids on the bottom. You are the parent and you must, without any hesitation or doubt, assert your authority. Kids must do what they are told and you must teach them to do so early.

In the first five years of life, children learn to do amazing things like walk and speak a language. My mother often said you should get your bluff in early. The first five years are so critical. During this time they learn behavior patterns which will last a lifetime and, by the time they are five years old, they should be minding you without question. They should know there are consequences for doing bad things, and you are the absolute authority.

So how early should you start? Many people believe the age of two is the magic number—it's often referred to as the "terrible twos." However, if you start to discipline your child before he is two, you just might find the "twos" are not so terrible. All kids are different, but they usually begin giving you clear signals it's time to start disciplining them at about twelve to eighteen months. Below are examples of clear signals your child might give you and how you should handle each situation.

The first example is the diaper change escape. A very common first opportunity to establish who's the boss is when a child doesn't want to hold still for a diaper change. If she rolls over and tries to crawl away while you are changing her diaper, your first response should be to pull her back and tell her no in a stern tone.

At this point, some children will lie there and resign themselves to being still. Mine never did. If she rolls over and begins to crawl away once again, this calls for a swat on the bare bottom or thigh. You must make it sting (just a little), or she won't feel it. Then pull her back and make her lie still until you are finished changing her. She will be surprised. Her eyes will get big, she'll gasp, draw a big breath and cry. You should ignore the crying, get on with changing the diaper and quickly move onto something else.

Most children will never try to escape during a diaper change again. What a delightful result. Additionally, the next time she does something you don't want her to do and you say no with the same tone, she may remember and not continue with it. However, there are exceptionally persistent ones. If you have a persistent child, you must be *more* persistent. You must react with the swat and firm *no* each time she attempts to escape a diaper change. On the surface, the diaper change escape does not seem like a huge crime deserving of such punishment. The issue is not the diaper change; it's the power struggle. It's about who is going to be in control.

Another way children let you know it's time to start disciplining them is when they arch their back and scream in defiance when you go to put them in their high chair, stroller or play pen. With my kids, it was always a high chair incident. This is a perfect opportunity to establish who is the boss early. Are you going to give in and not put them in the high chair? Lose this little battle and you're going to lose some more crucial ones down the road. Your response should be a quick swat on the rear or thigh, firmly telling them *no*, and putting them in the high chair in spite of their protests. Again, make it sting just a little or it will have no effect.

In addition to beginning discipline between the ages of twelve and eighteen months, it's also a good time to stop indulging your child's every request. When you bring home your newborn baby you are on call twenty-four hours a day in response to the baby's needs. You naturally get into the habit of jumping up and reacting every time the baby cries. Which is okay when the child is an infant but it cannot continue.

When children begin to walk and talk, you need to start putting on the brakes a little. Don't be so quick to jump up and satisfy every request. It's alright to tell them *no*, and it's okay if they cry about it. This doesn't make you a bad parent. Children need to learn they are not entitled to ordering you around like a servant. How much will children respect a parent who can be ordered around and manipulated so easily? If your child has an urgent need, tend to it immediately. But when he or she starts asking for things just to get you up out of your chair, or for the mere pleasure of seeing you do things for them, start saying *no*.

Notwithstanding the benefits discipline brings to children—providing them with a sense of security and teaching them right from wrong—life is so much easier when your kids do what they are told. Having control of my children gave me peace in my life. Because I was cool, calm and collected, I was a better and more effective parent. My home was free from yelling, counting to three, nagging and chaos. Little things which could have been big deals in a home with four children were a breeze. For example, at bedtime we only had to tell all four of them once to get their jammies on and get in bed. We would always go in later to tuck them in and give them a kiss, but we didn't have to tell them over and over to get ready for bed. Whenever we took them places, whether a restaurant, family get-together or mall, they made us proud.

Teaching kids to behave and respect your authority is critically important. As the parent you not only have the right, but the *duty*, to be the one who is in control. In order to get your bluff in early, begin to discipline at the first sign of resistance.

Rule Two—Be Consistent

Kids need structure and predictability. Lack of structure and predictability can cause children to become nervous and anxious and, as a result, very unhappy. Children need to know what the rules are. They find security in the fact the rules are always the same and you will always be there to enforce them. Be assured, however, they will test you to find out how far they can go, what they can do and what they can get away with. It is truly remarkable how much time and energy children will expend in their efforts to figure this out. The fact that they spend so much time testing is testament to just how important it is to them. It's a seemingly never-ending pursuit. The bottom line is you must always pass the test. If you discipline a child for something he did today, and he does the same thing tomorrow or next week or whenever, you must discipline him again.

Two-year-olds are famous for testing boundaries and checking to see if you are still there to enforce them. If your two-year-old throws a temper tantrum today and you respond by giving him two good swats on the rear end chances are good, because he is a two-year-old, he may try to throw a temper tantrum again within the next few days. You must be quick to put a stop to it when he tries it again. Another two or three good swats are in order.

If you fail to discipline him when he has his second tantrum, he will have learned nothing about throwing tantrums. He will be confused about why he was punished in the first place. If he has a tantrum today and you allow it, but tomorrow you spank him for throwing a tantrum, he will be just as confused. This type of inconsistent discipline will leave a child confused by not knowing what his boundaries are, and insecure by not knowing exactly what he is doing wrong to deserve the spankings.

Without consistency, discipline is ineffective. Any of the long-term benefits you hope to accomplish by disciplining your children will not be realized if you do not follow this rule. Establish boundaries you enforce with consistency. If you do, your children will be happier and more secure.

Rule Three—Don't Delay

It's important a child be corrected for bad behavior as soon as possible after it occurs. There is nothing more annoying than hearing someone issue threat after threat to a child who is not responding. A child soon learns just how long he can delay doing, or not doing, what mom says. If she typically asks one, two or even three times before she issues several threats, the child knows just how long to wait until she gets up to swat his behind. And if mom has never gotten up to swat his behind, he'll wait for whatever punishment is imminent (such as a timeout).

In this type of situation, by the time mom gets up she is angry and frustrated, which is never a good situation when correcting children. Swift, precise action by a calm, controlled mom or dad is what is required.

Ever hear this? "Michael, please come here. Michael, I said come here, come here now. Michael! Please come here now. Come on now Michael we have to get your shoes on so we can stop by the store and get something for dinner. Let's go. Michael, I'm going to count to three and you'd better . . . one, two, three! Okay, you're in trouble mister . . . blah, blah, blah!"

Here is how Michael's mom should have handled the situation. She should have said, "Michael, come here and get your shoes on." If Michael ignored her and failed to respond immediately, she should have walked over to him and warmed his butt with a few good swats followed with, "I said, come here." The element of surprise in this case would have a significant effect. The next time the need arose for Michael to come, the entire scenario would be much more peaceful and pleasant for everyone, including any onlookers. In the future,

Michael's mom will say, "Michael come here," and Michael will stop what he is doing and come immediately. Any onlookers will be utterly impressed. Additionally, some day Michael's quick obedience may save his life.

The story about Janette and April playing in the streambed illustrates the life-saving benefit of teaching kids to respond to you immediately. If I had allowed a behavior pattern to form that first I issued a command ("April and Janette, come here now!"), then spent five eternal minutes barking threats, my precious little girls would not be here today—and that is a fact.

One important aspect about this rule is the parent who is present is responsible for issuing swift justice when kids misbehave. Don't make the mistake of saying, "Wait until your father gets home." It's never a good idea to wait until dad gets home. Usually, the incident is forgotten by then and the child is never corrected. Besides, the dad shouldn't have to deal with a situation that happened while he was away.

Rule Four—Never Punish When You're Angry

Before I go into my explanation of this rule, we need to discuss the overall subject of anger. This is a story about a father who spanked his child because he was angry, not because it was part of a discipline program. This couple, friends of ours, rarely disciplined their children. One time I actually witnessed a spanking at their house. Their little girl had put something in the VCR and, consequently, it broke. My heart went out to the little girl who had never been punished for playing with the VCR before, she must have felt it was okay. Her father became angry because it was something which personally affected him. Replacement or repair of the VCR would cost him money. She did not get a spanking for playing with the VCR, she got spanked because her father was angry. He overreacted.

This next story relates to my theory child abuse is more likely to occur when there is lack of an appropriate discipline program which includes a firm hand on the rear end now and then. Recently, another well-known television daytime talk show featured mothers who were at the ends of their ropes. They were completely unable to cope with life at home with the kids. They showed a film of a three-year-old girl having the tantrum to beat all tantrums in a city park. Her mother was trying to get her into the stroller so they could go home. The child was red-faced, screaming and kicking—totally out of control. The mother was dragging her along on the ground by the arm.

Crying and sobbing on national television, the mother confessed she was afraid to be with the child because she felt like she was losing control and feared for the child's safety. An "expert" on the show suggested the child was reflecting her mother's anger and frustration. Furthermore, he said she was probably not suited to stay at home with her kids so she should go to work. What a cop-out this advice was! Not one word was mentioned about the lack of discipline for this poor child. If her mother had paddled her when she was much younger for disobedience and temper tantrums, the problem would not have escalated to the point where a small child was at risk.

Contrast this with how I raised my children. Between the ages of 12 and 18 months, I began the discipline program. I was relentless. I never let up and I never caved in. By the time they were three years old, they were disciplined. In the same situation in the park, I would have said, "Come on let's go," and that would be it. I never needed to get that physical—to grab an arm and try to drag a kid where I wanted them to go. The tantrum and the screaming and the dragging of a kid on the ground, to me, was much more violent than the few swats my kids got when they were only one year old. None of my children ever resisted my authority or acted so defiantly. I was, therefore, never pushed to the edge where I thought I would lose control and actually hurt them. They were never in any danger of me taking out my anger and frustration on them physically.

Never punish or spank a child when you are angry or not in control of your emotions. Anger and punishment have nothing to do with each other. When you punish a child, it should be because he needs it. It can never be because of your anger.

Imagine an anger scale with a range of one to ten, one being "mildly agitated" and ten being your "boiling point." When your child is doing something wrong, or your toddler is testing you (again), you should act when your anger is no more than three on the anger scale. Don't wait until you reach ten. Spanking or paddling should not be the last resort. If it is, you're probably too angry and shouldn't be punishing your child in that state of mind. If you get into the habit of acting while you are cool, calm and collected, a lot of good things will result. First, you won't lose your cool and, second, your child will learn you mean business. He will learn he will get paddled for doing a particular thing, not just because he has made you angry. There is a big difference. The difference is, if a child realizes he gets swatted because he has pushed your buttons, he also realizes he has a little power. I often see children invoke this kind of power over parents.

I don't mean to say your children should not ever see you are human. I believe it's healthy for them to know their parents do have emotions and sometimes get angry or upset. When you are angry, it's an opportunity for you to teach children restraint. As I'll explain later, one of the chief goals of my discipline program is to teach them self-control. When you get angry, consider it your opportunity to teach by example.

There are behaviors which justify good spankings (you'll find them in Chapter Five). When a child does those things, your reaction should be a calm deliberate application of punishment in accordance with your discipline program. If you find you are too angry to control yourself, either gain control of yourself or choose not to punish your child at all.

Rule Five—Always Follow Through With a Threat

My kids knew they better mind. They knew because I never failed to get up and swat their behinds if they didn't. I could go anywhere with my children and be confident they would obey any order. On many occasions I took all four of them into the grocery store with me. The baby would be in the baby seat of the shopping cart, and the other three would hold on to the cart so they didn't get separated from me. I had complete control. They knew they could not touch anything in the store without permission from me. If they reached for something, all I had to say was *no* and that would be the end of it. I also taught them not to ask for things when we were out shopping. If I had to indulge every desire they had at the grocery store, I'd spend a million dollars each time I went, not to mention the time it would take to get the shopping done. I made a trip to the grocery store with four children look easy. And it was because I had control of my kids. They were very good and they didn't get that way without the extra effort it took on my part. A very big part of that extra effort is following through with threats.

Always follow through with a threat. Idle threats will render you completely ineffective as far as discipline goes. I cringe when I hear parents threaten their kids. Most of the time I can predict what will happen— nothing. I wait to see if they will actually do what they are threatening to do, and I am always disappointed. It's not that I enjoy seeing kids punished, but it's so disappointing to see yet another parent failing to teach their children to mind them.

If you say something like, "If you touch that vase, I'm going to spank you," you have just made a promise you must keep. If your child reaches for the vase, you must follow through with the punishment you promised. If you threaten he will not get any ice cream if he doesn't finish his dinner, then don't let him have ice cream if he doesn't finish his dinner. I realize this is difficult for some people, but it is so important to stick to your guns. When you follow through with what you say, children learn *no* means *no*, and they learn to respect your authority without question.

Think about what it will be like when your children are teenagers if they have not learned to respect you. When kids reach their teens, the battle will begin between you and them on just how much freedom they are going to have. They are going to go out with friends, they will be going to parties, they will want to drive the minute they turn the legal age to do so. Without having any influence or control over your children up to this point, you will not magically have it now that they are teens, and this is when you will need it the most. Out of control teenagers are parents' nightmares. You will not be able to trust them to refuse drugs or alcohol, abide by curfews, drive safely and the list goes on and on.

I believe all parents want their children to become trustworthy teenagers. It's so easy. Draw the line, and if they cross that line, follow through with the consequences each and every time. The rewards you will reap will be well worth it. Your teenagers will respect you, and they will respect your rules. They will be responsible, honest and trustworthy. You will be proud of them and enjoy a mutually loving relationship. It's true. Believe me, I know first hand—both as a former teenager who respected my parents, and as the mother of four children who were respectful teenagers.

Respect is earned—not demanded. Teach your children they can count on your word and you will earn their respect. It all starts when they are very young, with your following through on every threat.

Rule Six—Never Apologize, Explain or Negotiate

Never apologize to your child for disciplining him. It's very normal to feel bad after paddling a child. Disciplining our children is something we must do as parents, but that doesn't mean we feel good about it, especially right afterwards. However, children do not need to know you feel bad about it. It diminishes the effectiveness of the punishment, and it sends them a confusing message they shouldn't have been punished at all.

What you *should* do is allow them to cry for ten minutes or so, but no longer. Then it's time for everyone to get over it. Children are usually over it in much less than ten minutes, which is healthy. What is not healthy is for you to drag out the whole affair by having a little talk about what he did wrong and then say you're sorry you had to spank him. My kids preferred I never brought the event up again—ever. If you have a child who wants to sit in your lap and talk about it then, by all means, that is what you should do. But if they are over it, you need to be over it too.

When Dad gets home from work, it's not a good idea to bring up all of the punishments of the day. If your child was already punished for what he did during the day, he doesn't need to be punished or admonished for it all over again when Dad gets home. What I used to do when John got home and asked how my day went was tell him all the fun and positive things we did. He heard nothing but the good stuff.

After paddling somebody for a wrongdoing, I would continue on with what I was doing before the incident happened. If the child kept crying too long, I would put an end to it and say something like, "Okay, that's enough, now go outside and play," or "Would you like to read a book with me?" They were always eager to stop crying and forget the whole thing. Usually, for the rest of the day they were especially good and didn't want to do anything to make me mad at them. They would often crawl into my lap for hugs and kisses. I would hug and kiss and tickle, but never went so far as to apologize.

In addition to not dragging out punishment, don't make the common mistake of thinking you owe your kids an explanation every time you turn around. It results in your child expecting an explanation to be offered before doing what he is told to do. The best explanation you can give your kids when you tell them to do something (or not do something) is "Because I said so." Otherwise, something as simple as telling them to put away their toys could end up being a negotiation, with the child perhaps agreeing to do it after manipulating you into promising a pay-off. The pay-off, or bribe, could be something like promising to take him out for ice cream if he hurries.

But what if there is a situation where you don't have time to explain or offer a bribe such as the one with Janette and April playing in the streambed? Do you think a three year old would understand an explanation about why she should get out of the way of rushing water? Would a two year old understand a lecture on the dangers of electricity so he won't stick something in an electrical outlet?

The truth is you do not owe children an explanation for any of your decisions and you certainly don't want to get into the habit of negotiating with them. It's a slippery slope which leads to loss of respect and authority. Just say *no* and leave it at that. If they want more, give them the old "Because I said so."

Rule Seven—Maintain a United Front

Parents need to realize how important it is for them to have what I call a *united front*—two parents who back each other up in all aspects related to raising their children. Ideally, the first step in establishing the united front takes place before having children. First, you agree on a discipline program, hopefully Back to Basics, then agree you will be united in the implementation of the program. You will become an invincible team with the same objective—raising spectacular kids.

Maintain a united front. In many households, one parent takes on the role of chief disciplinarian. Such was the case in my mother's house and in mine. This doesn't present any particular problem as long as the united front is maintained. My father rarely disciplined my brothers and me, but he also never interfered when my mother disciplined us. Most of the time he was at work, and when he came home he was very tired and just wanted to rest and enjoy his family. My mother was more than happy to take on the role of chief disciplinarian, as long as my father backed her up.

This story shows how important it is to back each other up.

Jessie, daughter of Jim and Sue, is three. Sue is a stay-at-home mom and the chief disciplinarian. When Jim came home from work in the evening, he was tired and just wanted to enjoy his family. However, he inadvertently would undermine Sue's attempts to discipline Jessie. For example, if Sue and Jessie were in the kitchen and Sue swatted Jessie for one reason or another, Jim would hop up and come into the kitchen and confront Sue as to what happened. It made Sue feel like she was being asked to explain herself in front of Jessie. The other thing he would do is when Jessie cried after being swatted, he would extend his arms and offer sympathy, making Sue feel like the bad guy. The overall effect was Jessie began to take advantage of this chink in the armor. She would mind Sue during the day, but when Daddy got home she began to misbehave, knowing he would come to the rescue.

What Sue did was have a talk with Jim after Jessie went to bed one night. She explained how he was undermining her authority. From then on, if Jim had a question about what happened, he would ask in private. When Jessie was disciplined he would back his wife up by saying to Jessie, "Mommy said *no*," or, "You must do what Mommy says." Jim and Sue reinforced their united front, and from then on Jessie settled down and stopped the habit of acting out after Daddy came home.

John and I were a good team. Much to the disappointment of our children at times, we had a bullet proof united front. Sometimes, as is normal for married people, one of us would not agree with a decision made by the other. In such cases we would never let on there was a disagreement, and the decision initially made was the one we both stood by. However, we would discuss it in private and try to work out how a similar situation would be handled in the future. We both knew keeping the united front was more important than disagreeing on something like whether Jeanine should be allowed to go to the movies with a friend on a school night or not. If I had given Jeanine permission to go, and John thought she should not be allowed to go, John would say nothing to Jeanine other than, "Bye, don't stay out too late." He would unequivocally support my decision. But he would talk to me about it later that night and give me the reasons he would have said no.

We would have a debate about it to be sure, as long as there were no children around to hear it.

When kids want something bad enough they start to invent clever ways to get it. John and I had enough foresight we were always able to stay one step ahead of the them. One of the things we did was to anticipate they would try to use one of us against the other. So when it happened, we jumped on it. For example, lets say Janette asked me if she could have some candy and I said no. That wasn't the answer she wanted so she went to her dad and asked him. He, not knowing I was already consulted, said yes. When I saw her with the candy I asked, "Who said you could have candy?" She said, "Dad said I could." This is manipulative and deceitful and nobody *ever* got away with it. Anybody who tried it got a spanking and we made darn sure they understood once they got an answer from one of us, they were never to go the other one and ask. By teaching them this one little thing, they knew they couldn't divide and conquer. It was a powerful thing.

If children learn they can undermine their parents' authority by running to another for sympathy, or going to the other parent to get a better answer to a question, they will most definitely take advantage of the situation. If you allow this to happen, it adversely affects Golden Rule 2—be consistent, and leads to losing respect for your authority. Remember, the success of any discipline program depends upon being able to control your child, which is directly related to his respect for your authority. By maintaining a united front you avoid inadvertently undermining your partner's authority and vice versa.

Make it Count

If you follow these rules, it will mean *less* actual punishment in the overall scheme of things. This set of rules is the difference between just wasting your time, going through the motions, making a lot of noise and putting up with a lot of nonsense, and actually getting results. They will ensure you will be teaching the lessons, earning the respect and becoming the effective parent you should be.

- By starting early you will instill in your child respect for your authority before it becomes a problem.

- By being consistent, your child will be more secure in knowing what to expect.

- By not delaying punishment, you will teach your child to obey your commands immediately, which could some day save his or her life.

- By making sure you are not angry when you punish, your child will know the punishment was because of *his* actions and not because of *your* anger.

- By always following through with your threats, your child will know he can count on you and *no* means *no*. Consequently, he will respect your authority without question.

- By never apologizing, explaining or negotiating, the lesson which was supposed to be learned will not be diminished or watered down.

- By maintaining a united front your authority will not be inadvertently sabotaged by your partner and vice versa.

These are the Seven Golden Rules, the third essential element in Back to Basics discipline.

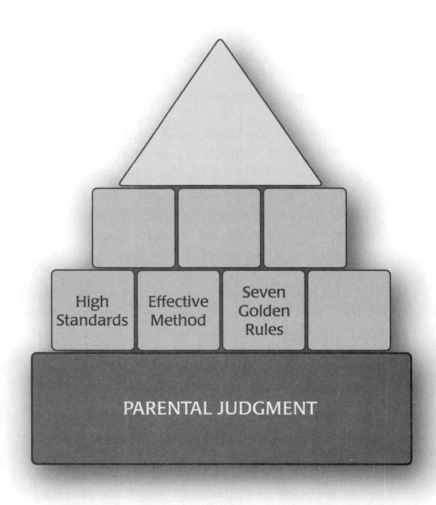

High
Standards

Effective
Method

Seven
Golden
Rules

PARENTAL JUDGMENT

5

Absolute No-Nos

" . . . whenever you discipline a child, it's important you do it for the right reasons, because the character of your child is at stake."

The Fourth Essential Element in Back to Basics Discipline

It's time to review what we've discussed so far. We've covered High Standards, using the most Effective Method of discipline and the Seven Golden Rules. Now, I will show you whenever you discipline a child, it's important you do it for the right reasons, because the character of your child is at stake.

Certain behaviors rob your children of the ability to develop traits necessary to form good character. A discipline program which includes a "no tolerance" policy toward those behaviors is the key to success. I call those behaviors the *Absolute No-Nos*, and they are: disobedience, disrespect, temper, dishonesty and aggression.

Disobedience

The opposite of *disobedience* is obedience. The gift you give your child when you teach him obedience is responsibility. Responsibility, by definition, is the ability to distinguish between right and wrong. It is an element of maturity, the special something that gives a person ownership of their actions. When a child is corrected for being disobedient, they learn there are things which are right and things which are wrong. They also learn there are consequences for actions, from which they learn to think before they act. Thinking before acting is the thought process of considering what the result for a certain action will be, then making a decision based on the expected result. For example, if a child knows the consequence for not obeying her mother when she tells her to put her toys away will result in a paddling, the child will choose to obey. As she gets older, she will apply this thought process in everything she does and it will become second nature for her.

Alternatively, a person who has not learned to consider the consequences of actions beforehand will naturally do whatever pleases them at any given moment. Such people are prone to making decisions based on emotions and irrational wants and desires rather than making sound, thoughtful decisions based on probable outcomes. They are immature and impulsive and always have an excuse when things go wrong. They go through life believing the rules are for everybody else, not them.

Disobedience is to resist authority, to refuse or fail to obey. Disobedience is defiance, and it takes many forms: inaction, action, spoken words and attitude. Let's look at some examples of each.

Karen has a five-year-old daughter, Jennifer. One night she tells Jennifer to put her toys away because it's almost bedtime. Jennifer doesn't want to stop playing and put her toys away so she ignores her mother and continues playing. This is defiance by inaction.

If Jennifer reacted by looking at her mother as if to say, "I challenge you to make me put my toys away," and reached in the toy box to get more toys out, this would be defiance by action.

If Jennifer turned around and said, "No, I don't *want* to put my toys away," obviously this would be defiance by spoken words. Defiance can also be in the form of throwing a fit, crying and whining. Karen shouldn't tolerate Jennifer's attempts to put the toys away with a bad attitude. If she threw the toys in the toy box in anger, or if she decided to go about it very slowly, Jennifer should get a few firm swats without any hesitation. Anything short of Jennifer stopping what she is doing and beginning to put her toys away compliantly should not be tolerated.

The best way to teach your child to be responsible is to never let them get away with *any* act of disobedience or defiance. Here are some ways the gift of responsibility will benefit your child for the rest of his or her life. When you send your little one off to school, he will already possess a sense of right and wrong. He will follow directions and obey rules. Consequently, he will sit still and listen to the teacher; do his homework assignments and virtually be a model student. Any child who can sit still, listen and do what they are told will learn. In fact, learning is a breeze for such children. None of their energy will be focused on challenging the teacher, goofing off in class to get attention or any other behaviors which detract from the learning environment.

When your child becomes an adult, his sense of right and wrong will become even stronger providing him the basis for success in everything he does. At work, he will show up on time and do his job, two basic ingredients for a successful career. His boss, co-workers and employees will know they can count on him. Any employer knows all too well how valuable such an employee is. Look at the top of the organization chart in any business and that's where you will find many people who possess the gift of responsibility.

Finally, your child will enjoy such wonderful things life has to offer such as social acceptance, lasting friendships and meaningful relationships. He will be loved and admired for his convictions, thoughtfulness and dependability.

Disrespect

The opposite of *disrespect* is respect. The gift you give your child when you teach him to be respectful is reverence. Reverence, by definition, is a feeling of deep respect and admiration. You, the parent, will be the first authority figure your child will encounter. If you do not have his respect, you have deprived him of a hero, a role model, someone who makes him say to himself, "I want to grow up and be just like that."

Respect for your parents is something every kid should have. My mother never let me get away with anything. She was a rock, and I respected her for it. She is my hero. Had I been able to walk all over her, I'm not so sure I would be the person I am today. The thought of disappointing her kept me out of trouble when I was a teenager. By then, I wasn't afraid of getting a spanking, but I *was* afraid of her disapproval. That kind of respect for a parent is what teenagers need to help them make the right choices.

The same principle applies to all authority figures in a kid's life. If he respects and admires his teacher, he is going to learn more from that teacher, he is going to enjoy that particular class and he will try harder to earn that teacher's praise.

A child will not respect you just because you are his parent, nor will he respect you because you tell him he should. Teaching children respect, or earning their respect, starts with fear. Sounds a little harsh, right? But it's Nature's way of instilling respect in every living being. My mother used to call it "healthy fear." Believe me, she instilled lots of healthy fear in us kids. Along the way, that healthy fear somehow turned into respect. I can't tell you how it happened. I know my friends, whose mothers were permissive and let their kids walk all over them, did *not* respect their mothers.

Disrespect takes many forms so you have to be on the lookout for it. It's bad attitude, talking back and other subtle things like giving you a dirty look or interrupting you when you're talking to another adult. You teach your child respect by not letting them get away with showing any disrespect, in any form.

Bad attitude is both verbal and physical. When my brothers and I were young, if my mother told one of us to do something we didn't want to do, she wouldn't let us show our grief. For example, one time she told my brother, Dick, to take out the trash. He frowned and sighed and headed for the trash can in the kitchen with his shoulders slumped down as if he was really inconvenienced by having to get up and do something. She surprised him with a few hard swats on the rear end and told him, "And smile about it!" He got the message. He straightened up, wiped the scowl off of his face and took the trash out as fast as he could as if it was a privilege. That's usually all it took. We were quick to learn Mom wasn't going to put up with any bad attitude.

Today, we still joke about it. When we ask Dick to do something for us we make sure we tell him he has to smile about it. The truth is Dick, now a grown man, is one of the most generous and giving souls on Earth. There isn't anything he won't do for anyone, but he especially takes pleasure in doing things for Mom.

Naturally, I learned this technique from my mother so my kids were taught when I asked them to do something for me, they'd better smile about it. It lightens the mood, gets kids to stop taking themselves so serious and it makes them mindful of their attitudes.

Be wary of the dirty look. Don't let your child ever get away with giving you a dirty look. It's pure disrespect. It's the same thing as telling you to go to hell. If she has that look on her face, I guarantee that's what she's thinking. The dirty look is a definite no-no.

One of the most unattractive things in this world is a child who talks back to his parents. Talking back is impudent and disrespectful. My mother would refer to someone who talked back as a "smart mouth." She never cut us any slack when it came to talking back. An example of talking back would be if Jennifer, after being told to put her toys away, turned to her mother and said, "I don't want to" or, "I'm too busy," or, "In a minute." Of course, as children get older, if they have been allowed to talk back and have a smart mouth, it just gets worse. They argue and fight with their parents and they won't take no for an answer. Talking back also includes the never-ending game of getting the last word in.

When I was about thirteen I had a friend I just loved to spend time with, but I hated going over to her house because of the way she talked to her mother. I would cringe when she talked to her mother with such disrespect. She would tell her mother to shut up, leave the room and worse. I finally got to the point where I would make my friend promise me she would be nice to her mother if I came over. She would agree. And I would warn her, "If you say one mean thing to your mom, I'm leaving." I actually did leave a couple of times. I just couldn't take it.

Another subtle form of disrespect is when a child interrupts adults when they are in conversation. Many parents get into the habit of stopping a conversation because their kid just came into the room to ask for something like a drink of water. I always told my children if they interrupted me when I was talking to another grown-up, somebody had better be bleeding. They were taught to come in to the room and wait until there was a pause in the discussion. They still weren't allowed to speak unless I looked at them and asked, "What is it?" I could tell from the looks on their faces if there was a real emergency. Most of the time it was a silly little request which could wait.

Interrupting adults talking doesn't seem like such a bad thing. But by not allowing my children to do it, I taught them a couple of lessons in addition to respect and consideration. One, they learned to be patient. They learned to wait until I looked at them before they could speak. Two, they learned the world didn't revolve around them twenty-four hours a day. This also taught them humility. Here you have a whole package of lessons wrapped up in one rule!

Don't let bad attitude be a habit in your home. Be on the lookout for all forms of disrespect and nip it in the bud. The entire Home Environment will be more pleasant and your children will respect you. Here is how his respect for you will have a lasting positive affect. He will have a hero. He will learn from you and want to be like you and have your values. He will respect other authority figures, an essential quality which will help him in school or his job. As a teenager, when he is eventually pressured by his peers to do all sorts of unseemly things, he'll think about the affect it would have on you and use better judgment. He will want to be better at everything he does because he will want you to be proud of him. Do you think he would care about what you thought of him if he did not respect you? That's where it all comes from.

Temper

The opposite of a *bad temper* is temperance. The gift you give your child when you teach him temperance is self-control.

We have all seen them—the screaming, out-of-control toddlers in a store or super market. The parents are so embarrassed they don't know what to do. Most of the time they ignore the tantrum because if they actually acknowledge their child having a big fit in the store, they might have to do something about it. The problem is parents get into the habit of indulging their children in order to avoid confrontation which usually comes in the form of a big fit.

It all starts at home. For example, if little three-year-old Steven asks his mother for some juice, she jumps up to get it. In fact, she is so in the habit of jumping up to get Steven everything he asks for, it becomes automatic. At the same time, Steven learns to expect this kind of catering. If for some reason Steven's mother tells him no, he throws himself on the floor and screams, and this works almost 100% of the time for Steven. Steven's mother chooses to comply with *all* of Steven's requests just so she doesn't have to deal with his temper. But allowing this behavior pattern to form is a very bad idea.

Realistically, it isn't going to be possible to give Steven everything he wants on demand. For instance, when Steven's parents take him with them to do some shopping, they may be out of the Home Environment but Steven still believes he must get everything on demand. If he reaches for a toy which is too expensive, they may have to tell him no. This brings on a temper tantrum because that's how he has been taught to get his way, and it has always worked. Since they don't know what to do about it, they ignore the behavior and do nothing.

Here is what Steven's mother should be doing at home. She should be telling Steven no now and then. And if he throws himself on the floor and screams, she should warm his bottom with a good spanking.

It's okay for you to tell your children no. Don't be afraid of the confrontation. If it happens, deal with it. It's not only okay to tell your children no, it's okay if they cry about it for a little while. But they should *not* be allowed to throw a temper fit. If your child has a hard time being told *no*, it means you need to use the word more often. In fact, you should practice telling him *no* at home, while teaching him to not throw a fit, until he has learned this important lesson: to control his temper and accept *no* for an answer. Once in a while, if your child asks for something and it's not critical he or she have it instantly, tell them no without any apologies or explanations. In other words, bring it on... bring on that tantrum and begin teaching the lessons. The more you do this at home, the sooner they learn hearing the word *no* won't kill them. You will be able to take your child places in public and not find yourself in the same situation as Steven's parents, with an out-of-control toddler and no clue as to how to deal with it.

I started teaching my children when they were one year old they were not allowed to show their tempers. By the time they were two, it never crossed my mind, until I went out and saw other people's kids getting away with it. Whenever that happened, my kids would even notice. They would look at me in utter shock, as if to say, "Mom! That kid is really being bad!"

A person who has not been taught to control himself faces difficulty in life. Life is tough and there are always going to be challenging and frustrating situations. There are more constructive ways to deal with problems and hardships than to throw a fit. Nobody should be allowed to throw a tantrum, mistreat others, throw things, break things or do any of the things people do when they are angry. I don't believe anyone, child or adult, who has a bad temper should be excused because they are young, have red hair, are not feeling well, are having a bad day or for any other reason. There is simply no excuse.

Here's how the gift of self-control will be an asset to your child for life. As a child, self-control will allow him to achieve emotional maturity. Emotional maturity will be helpful in relationships, social situations and sports activities. Throughout life he will be a problem solver rather than a whiner. He will possess inner strength, which is only possible through the ability to control his emotions so he can think clearly and concisely. All energies will be used for positive things such as problem solving rather than for negative things like complaining and huffing and puffing. Others will be attracted to him for his mature, cool demeanor and his optimism. Anyone who is self-disciplined has the ability to overcome adversity—what a powerful gift.

Dishonesty

The opposite of *dishonesty* is truthfulness. The gift you give your child by teaching him not to lie is honesty.

My mother used to say, "There's nothing I despise more than a liar." Mom had a way of boiling things down to simple terms we could understand. To me, that said it all. She made it sound like a liar was the lowest form of life on earth, and I never wanted her to think of me like that.

One reason I never tried lying to my parents is probably because my brother did once, and that time my dad spanked him. (Usually my mother was the disciplinarian and had it all taken care of while dad was at work, but this time my dad took care of business). This particular instance is still referred to by my family as "the Blueberry Muffin Caper." My brothers were about nine and seven years old at the time and I was six. Mom had baked some blueberry muffins and set them on the counter in the kitchen to cool. They were going to be served with dinner that night. It came to be one or two muffins were missing by the time dinner rolled around. Mom asked the three of us kids if we ate the muffins and we all denied it. Since there wasn't anybody else in the house, my parents knew somebody was lying. My dad decided to get to the bottom of things. It wasn't that the blueberry muffins were all that important, but he knew somebody had lied and he wanted to make sure whoever it was didn't get away with it. It was time to teach us all a lesson. He called us into the room with his serious, scary tone of voice which implied somebody was in trouble. He lined us up in a row and told us on the count of three we were to stick out our tongues. He said whoever ate the blueberry muffins would have a blue tongue. Even though I was innocent, I was terrified my tongue was going to be blue. My dad got to "two" and at that point my brother, Mitch, started to cry and confessed immediately. Dick and I were off the hook. Dad didn't need to see anybody's tongue. He didn't even know if there would be a blue tongue, he was banking on scaring the truth out of one of us, and it worked. Mitch got his spanking that night and I knew, from that moment on, I was never going to lie to my parents.

One year, my sister-in-law gave a surprise birthday party for my brother, Mitch. It was his fiftieth birthday. She invited lots of relatives and friends and people he worked with, including his boss. We all got to take turns at the podium and most of us roasted him good. But the best part about the entire evening was when Mitch's boss took the podium. He didn't have a joke to tell or anything funny to say. He just proceeded to tell all of us what an honest guy Mitch was, and he never met anyone with so much integrity. Of course, those of us who know Mitch were not surprised. He is one of the most honest, sincere guys you'll ever meet in your whole life. It was a heartfelt and very touching moment. I think it all goes back to the Blueberry Muffin Caper.

When you are an honest person, and people know it, it can sure come in handy. By the time I was in the seventh grade, my mother was confident I was not a liar. She knew I wouldn't lie to save my own skin. She stuck up for me when the school librarian was harassing me about a book which she said I had never returned. I explained to my mother I did check the book out, but after reading it, I returned it to the library. The librarian kept sending threatening notes home saying if I did not return the book I would have to pay for it. When Mom saw how upset I was, she went down to the school with me in tow. She spoke with the librarian and stated, "Janet says she returned the book and I believe her. My daughter does not lie." My mother told the librarian to stop bothering me. The librarian did not back down and the matter was left unresolved. Lo and behold, a few days later the librarian called my mother and apologized because the book had been there all along. My mother made the librarian apologize to me personally. How lucky I was my mother believed me. I was so impressed with the fact she confronted the librarian on my behalf and never once questioned whether I was telling the truth or not, even when it was my word against a grown-ups. I was truly amazed.

Now that I am a parent, I see the whole incident from my mother's point of view, and I can see how she must have thought how wonderful it was to have a child she could trust so explicitly. When the librarian called to say the book had turned up, my mother must have felt so smug.

I've never forgotten those lessons about lying. I made my opinion clear to my kids as soon as they could understand, the lowest form of life on earth was a liar. I could always trust my children to tell me the truth, even when they had to admit to something they did wrong. They still got punished for the wrongdoing, but not as severely as if they had lied about it and I had found out. You can't let them off the hook if they admit to a wrongdoing. It wouldn't take a kid long to learn they could do just about anything and get away with it as long as they told the truth about it. You still must punish them. But you must make it clear the punishment will be more severe if they lie about it too.

My guess is I don't have to tell you the benefits of teaching your kids honesty. People who live their life in the light—those honest souls who always tell the truth—need not go through life looking over their shoulder, waiting to see if someone is going to discover the truth about one of their lies. People who are honest with others naturally are more honest with themselves, which is another important element in reaching emotional maturity. Honesty is the best policy, and a precious gift.

Aggression

In the context of behavior in children, the opposites of *aggression* are kindness and understanding. The gift you give your child for teaching him not to hurt others is compassion.

This is a no-brainer. What amazes me is I see parents who are so completely tolerant of their kids hurting other kids. Just saying, "No-no," and giving them a timeout is utterly irresponsible on the part of a parent. Even those who don't believe in spanking on general principle need to seriously consider a few firm swats for this one. A child who bites and kicks and hits other children needs a good paddling. This is just plain meanness and should not be tolerated.

It's normal for a very young child who is just learning to play with other children to do something like push or hit another child if that child reaches for his favorite toy. When a child does this, he deserves a little swat on the rear end. Even if it *is* his favorite toy, he should not be allowed to hurt other people. However, when children get older, I would say around five years old, and they are physically aggressive to other children and/or their parents, there is a deeper problem. It's probably not a matter of learning to share their toys. More likely, they are crying out for discipline. They're frustrated and angry and need a firm hand to get them to settle down. Remember, children want to feel safe and loved. This kind of angry child is yearning for security.

Life's greatest joy is about loving and being loved. Without compassion, neither one is possible. Teach your children to be kind and thoughtful. They will learn to be less self-centered and more compassionate. The gift of compassion will bring out all of the sweet, loving attributes your child naturally possesses. His kindness and understanding will enhance his friendships and relationships. His compassion will make him a truly lovable, therefore happier, person.

Mishaps and House Rules

You need to get a firm grasp of what is important. For example, spilled milk is not important. If your three-year-old was learning to eat at the table with the grown ups and accidentally spilled his milk, I don't believe he needs a spanking. After all, it was just an accident.

You undoubtedly will have your own particular house rules. Whenever your house rules are broken, discipline is justified, but be sure the punishment fits the crime. Usually, a broken house rule is not as serious as the Absolute No-Nos. For a broken house rule I would do something less severe like taking away something they like such as watching a favorite TV show or having a favorite treat after supper.

This story illustrates how punishment fits the crime. When I was growing up my parents had a house rule when my brothers and I were out playing in the neighborhood, if we heard my father whistle we were to come home right away. My father had a very loud, distinctive whistle which could be heard up and down our street. An important aspect of this rule was if you didn't hear the whistle, you were out of range and too far from the house. If you didn't hear the whistle and come home, it was your fault and you were in trouble. If we failed to return home at the sound of the whistle, we didn't get to go outside and play the next day. We loved playing outside with the neighborhood kids, and from then on we were careful to stay close enough to home to hear my father's whistle. This punishment fit the crime.

Of course you have to be able to determine whether the house rule was broken inadvertently or in defiance with deliberate malice. It all depends on how serious the matter is. You need to use your own judgment on a case-by-case basis.

When my daughter, Janette, was only two years old she got hold of a crayon and decorated the kids' playroom walls. As hard as I tried, I never seemed to keep her older siblings' crayons out of her reach. She was too little to know it was wrong to mark on the walls. When I discovered the artwork, Janette didn't get a spanking. I just gave her a little rag and had her help me wash it off the wall. She wasn't much help, but she got the message it wasn't supposed to be there. This kind of stuff never mattered to me. The walls of my house weren't all that important. My kids were, and that's why I was mostly concerned with the Absolute No-Nos instead of those little mishaps.

Stay Focused on the Big Picture

Some people seem to be confused about what they should tolerate and what they should not tolerate when it comes to their children's behavior. Many seem to be less concerned with the Absolute No-Nos, and more concerned about the little things—like my friends' mothers who were so concerned about a clean bedroom and not the least bit concerned about talking back. Stay focused on the big picture.

- If you discipline your child for *disobedience*, you teach him *responsibility*.
- If you discipline your child for *disrespect*, you teach him *respect*.
- If you discipline your child for *temper*, you teach him *self-control*.
- If you discipline your child for *dishonesty*, you teach him *honesty*.
- If you discipline your child for *aggression*, you teach him *compassion*.

Responsibility, respect, self-control, honesty and compassion are the fundamental character traits which lead to living good lives, being good people and doing good things—the long-term goals of discipline (see Chapter Two). A no-tolerance policy toward the Absolute No-Nos is the fourth essential element in Back to Basics discipline.

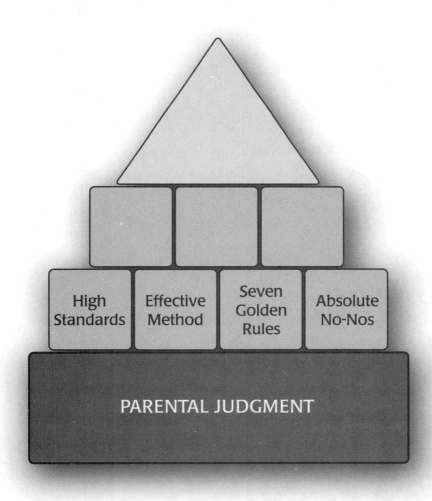

High Standards | Effective Method | Seven Golden Rules | Absolute No-Nos

PARENTAL JUDGMENT

6

Separate Worlds

" . . . some things are off limits to them—
and some things are so much sweeter
when they're not so easy to come by."

The Fifth Essential Element
in Back to Basics Discipline

Let's review. We've covered High Standards, using the most Effective Method of discipline, the Seven Golden Rules and the Absolute No-Nos. Those four are going to get you fantastic results. However, don't stop here! I am about to give you some excellent advice.

I have a theory there should be a distinct line drawn between the "kid world" and the "adult world." The privileges of adulthood are extremely attractive, and most children just can't wait to indulge themselves in the trappings of adulthood. Staying up late, eating what you want, going where you want, not having to ask permission and watching whatever you want on television are some of the big attractions. One of the biggest struggles parents have is keeping all of this under control, but you can do it by taking a few simple measures.

What Are They Seeing and Hearing?

Be aware of what your children are exposed to. What they hear and what they see should be carefully monitored. Leaving the television on all day long, for example, and tuned to a 24-hour news channel is not a good thing, but neither are daytime soap operas. Even if children do not appear to be watching the television, they hear it. Various adult subjects are discussed on television which are not appropriate for little children. If your child is having nightmares, you might try turning off the TV. When my kids were little, I would let them watch a few cartoons in the morning, then the TV would be turned off until after dinner. I believe this contributed to the fact my children were never addicted to television and never became couch potatoes. With the television off, they were more likely to spend their time playing outside, doing hobbies, playing sports, reading, doing homework and any of the other things you would rather see them doing other than sitting in front of a television in the middle of the day. After dinner I would make sure if they watched television, it would be suitable family programming. Be careful, a great deal of television programming has become raunchy. Many of the programs shown in an early time slot once reserved for family viewing have crossed the line. The language and subject matter are not appropriate for little children so it's important to select programming wisely. The same goes for movies they attend.

Another thing to be aware of is what children hear when adults gather together. It's not healthy for kids to hang around and listen to adult conversation. It may expose them to subject matter which could cause them to have unfounded worries and fears. They are not emotionally mature enough to handle listening to adult conversations. What you *should* do is send them outside or to their bedrooms to play. By doing this you protect their little psyches from potential emotional disturbances in addition to reminding them they are children—not adults. Let them know they can't indulge themselves in adult behavior and adult conversation. I would be completely annoyed when my friends would let their kids sit in the room and listen to what the grown-ups were talking about. Sometimes their children would join the conversation without being invited, and I would think to myself how incredibly bold and improper it was.

Rules Which Separate the Kids From the Adults

My mother was brilliant at making up house rules simply for the purpose of separating the kids from the grown-ups. For instance, she had a saying that See's Candy was too good for kids. If there was a box of See's in the house, we would never ask for some because we actually believed it was only for adults. It wasn't that we couldn't have candy—we could, as long as it wasn't something as expensive as See's. She would let us have the less expensive stuff like Tootsie Rolls or M&Ms. Once in a while Mom would take out the See's box and motion to us to come over and pick out a piece. This was such a treat! We would take forever deciding which one we wanted because there wouldn't be a second chance if you picked something you didn't like. This taught us some things were just for adults (and for kids on special occasions). We would never expect or assume we could have something like See's. It put us in our places, and also made something small like picking out a piece of candy a very special event.

Naturally, John and I thought this was a smart rule so See's Candy was off-limits to kids most of the time in our house. Once in a while John would dole it out to one of the kids when the others weren't around to make him or her feel special.

Another thing that drives me crazy about some children is when they help themselves to Mom's or Dad's coffee or beer. I never thought there was anything cute about it, and therefore didn't let my kids help themselves to such things without asking. Actually, they knew better than to ask because I wouldn't have said yes.

Decision Making

Some parents don't realize they ask their small children to make too many decisions. A two-year-old does not need to be consulted about what they want to wear, where they want to go and what restaurant they want to eat in. It amazes me how many mothers ask their toddlers to make those decisions. They are just little kids! It's not fair to burden them with decisions you should be making. It also isn't a good idea to share your power with a child. In their eyes, you should be a strong, decisive grown-up who is in charge. As they get older and demonstrate certain levels of maturity, it's healthy to allow them to begin to make decisions. For example, it's okay to allow a seven-year-old to choose between the red dress or the blue dress. But keep the choices limited and simple. By the time she is thirteen, she can decide what to wear as long as she uses good judgment.

Most teenagers struggle for independence and one of the most important expressions of independence is being able to make decisions. This is a critical time in a child's life and balancing their desires for more independence and your responsibility as a parent is a delicate undertaking. The point is, if you have young children, *you* make the decisions.

Your Space—Your Stuff

It's healthy for your children to know you are a human being—a real person with feelings. Teach them to respect you *and* your things. When I was little my father had his recliner chair which nobody sat in but him. If he was gone it was okay to sit in his chair, but when he walked into the room you'd better not wait for him to ask you to move.

John and I had the same rule in our house. We both had our favorite chairs, which the kids vacated immediately when we came home. In fact, we taught our children to always offer their chairs to an adult who enters the room. It became a habit for them to do this wherever they went.

We also had a rule about Pepsi. The kids weren't allowed to have sodas when they were little and they knew the Pepsi was off limits. When they got into their teens, however, it was okay and everyone could pretty much help himself to what was in the refrigerator. And that is why we adopted the Pepsi Rule, which was a rule my mom imposed on my brothers and me when we were still at home. The rule went like this: Thou shalt not drink the last Pepsi. That way, if John or I went to the refrigerator to get a Pepsi, there would actually be one there. If he or I had drank the last Pepsi, that would be okay. But if he or I were denied a Pepsi because a kid drank it, there was hell to pay. This was such a good rule we made it apply to the last cookie, last brownie and last piece of cake.

The funny thing is, when our son, Ken, moved out and got his own apartment, he confessed to me he couldn't bring himself to drink the last Pepsi or eat the last cookie even in his own home! He's married now and I'll bet my daughter-in-law, Kristi, likes this rule. I have a feeling they will impose the Pepsi Rule in their house when they have children.

Another more serious rule we had was kids didn't get to sleep in Mom and Dad's bed. As warm and cuddly as this seems, it's a bad habit. If we had let just one of them climb in bed and stay there the whole night with us, it would have been the last time either one of us got a good night's sleep. As a matter of survival we had to make this a steadfast rule. It was also a way of letting them know there were limits to what they could help themselves to. It was healthy for them to respect our bedroom and our bed. Of course, we would let everybody come in and join us in the mornings, which would usually end up in a tickle fight. When they got older, they soon learned it would end up with us making them go get us our coffee. That was a good deterrent right there!

Sometimes, in the middle of the night, somebody would have a scary dream and come into our room. We would usually comfort them and put them back in bed. If it was really scary, we let them get a sleeping bag and pillow and sleep in our room on the floor. I know it sounds cold, but if they truly had a scary dream this was a great offer to them. As I said, if we had allowed them to climb in bed with us, we would *never* have gotten a good night's sleep again. Don't let kids have free access to your bedroom or your bed. There are just some limits you have to set.

Teaching your kids to be considerate and think of others first is a good lesson for them and rules about your space and your stuff are a good place to start.

Preserving Childhood

Childhood is magical—children don't worry about the future or obsess about the past, they just live in the moment. Because it is such a special time, we should not let children grow up too fast. Plus, it's important for them to learn they just can't have it all, some things are off limits to them, and there are some things which are so much sweeter when they're not so easy to come by. Of course, we want to preserve their innocence as long as we can.

Be mindful of what your children are exposed to in the adult world, save some privileges for when they grow up and make them respect your things. If you do, they will enjoy childhood a little bit longer. You'll find yourself enjoying it too!

Maintaining Separate Worlds is the fifth essential element in Back to Basics discipline.

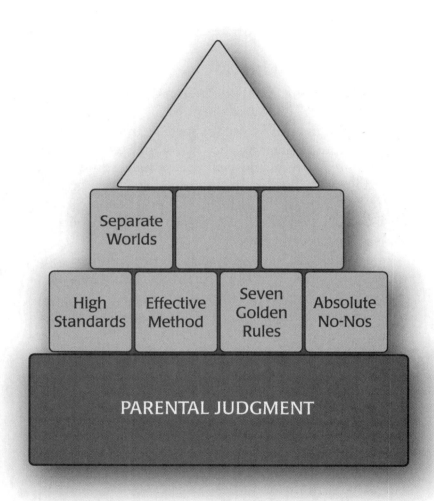

7

Sibling Relationships

"Brothers and sisters who can rely upon
each other throughout life for uncondi-
tional love and support are truly blessed."

The Sixth Essential Element
in Back to Basics Discipline

Let's review again. We've covered High Standards, using the most Effective Method of discipline, the Seven Golden Rules, the Absolute No-Nos, and maintaining Separate Worlds. But the discipline program is not yet complete. Sibling relationships play a large part in the overall development and happiness of children. Therefore, I just couldn't leave this part out.

One of the most important things parents can do is foster and nurture the relationships their children have with each other. Siblings have a great deal in common. They share the same parents, the same home and family traditions and they share childhood memories (both good and bad). Brothers and sisters who can rely upon each other for unconditional love and support are truly blessed. Ideally, you raise your children with their Sibling Relationships intact so they will always have each other. In addition to giving them the gift of strong character discipline brings, the gift of unspoiled Sibling Relationships is something which shouldn't be overlooked. Here are some tips.

Age Has Privilege

When there is more than one child in a family, the dynamics of who was born first comes in to play. Throw out those old beliefs about everything in life being fair. Fairness is quite a different animal when it comes to kids and you need to understand how important it is to see fairness through the eyes of your children.

The first trap to watch out for is thinking you must treat all of your children exactly the same (for example, making everyone go to bed at the same time). Each child is different because of genetics, gender and personality. They're also different from each other because of the order in which they were born. There is the first born, those in between and, of course, the baby. All must be treated differently according to their birth order.

Age matters when it comes to privilege. Your firstborn needs to enjoy special recognition for being the oldest. It won't take much effort on your part, but you must give them this special recognition. One way is to put them to bed in order according to their ages. Staying up later than their younger siblings was a big deal to our older children, even if it was only twenty minutes longer. There was a time when bedtime was staggered twenty minutes apart from the oldest to the youngest.

Now you're worried about explaining this to the younger children, right? It's simple. Your answer to the question, "Mom, why does Kevin get to stay up later than me?" is, "Because Kevin is older than you." Period. That's the entire explanation. You need to hang tough on this one—offer no apologies, stick to your guns and don't feel bad about it.

The oldest child is burdened with more responsibility. They are often called upon to help the younger ones do all kinds of things. Because they are older and available, they end up watching the younger ones for you. Sometimes, just for a minute while you take a shower or check the mailbox or longer, so you can run to the store.

Older children have more chores to do, and in many cases their chores are more difficult than those the younger kids are expected to do. Since we all tend to rely on our older children more than the others, we can offset this burden with a few extra privileges like staying up later. I can't tell you how much mileage you will get out of this one. Older children love this privilege. If you provide little extras for them, you will avoid planting the seeds of resentment in your oldest child. The seeds of resentment are dangerous in a couple of ways. They will resent you for not acknowledging their status as the oldest child, and they will resent their siblings for a very long time without knowing why.

Are They Really Twins?

If you don't have twins, you shouldn't be treating your children as such. A case in point: Sharon and Susan were sisters, born less than two years apart. Their mother, Irene, thought it was cute to dress them exactly alike when they were little, but she didn't stop there. At Christmas they got the exact same things. If

Sharon got a Barbie Doll, so did Susan—the exact some one. They enjoyed the same privileges at the exact same ages. When they were older, they were both allowed to do grown-up things like wear pumps or panty hose. Sharon, the oldest, was cheated out of her recognition for being the oldest. She resented the fact her younger sister got to do everything she did, even though Susan was younger. Irene should have first allowed Sharon to wear pumps, say when she was thirteen, and made Susan wait until she was thirteen before allowing her to wear pumps. Everything else was the same as well. . . their bedtime, when they were allowed to date, when they were allowed to wear lipstick and even their curfews.

Sharon, now a grown woman, still carries resentment for her little sister, and probably doesn't even know why. From the time she was a teenager Sharon began to rebel against her parents and resent her sister. It caused a lot of strife in the family, which they still struggle with some twenty years later. It wasn't fair to Sharon or Susan to treat them like twins. Susan probably doesn't have a clue why her sister hates her. I'm sure Irene thought treating them the same was the fair thing to do. If she had known the damage it was doing to the girls' relationship, she might have thought twice about it.

Sibling Cruelty

Sibling cruelty is when a child, usually the older one, is allowed to physically brutalize younger sisters or brothers—those who are too young to defend themselves. This usually happens because the older child was never disciplined and, as a result, is the one who is actually in control of the house. Mom and dad are actually afraid to discipline their unruly older child, and take the path of least resistance by expecting the younger, defenseless children to endure the brutality. They are expected to put up with such things as having toys grabbed from their hands, painful pinches and whacks on the head with hard objects. It doesn't matter how many times parents look the other way or tell the younger child to toughen up, it doesn't make this right.

Tag Alongs

Another way to spoil a sibling relationship is to force an older child to play with a younger one. I recall seeing it happen at my friends' houses when I was little. Their unhappiness was obvious when their mothers would open up the bedroom door, shove a little sister in and say, "Let Janie play too." Nothing creates resentment and hatred for a sibling like being forced to let them in their room when they have friends over. I know parents do it to make life easier for themselves, but I can't think of any time it's a good idea. As tempting as it seems, avoid making this mistake. I never forced my older children to play with their younger siblings. As a result, there were times they would willingly play with their younger siblings. When it was their idea, it was so much sweeter for everyone involved.

Tattle Tales

Another pitfall to watch out for is allowing children to tattle on each other. As much as a parent wants to know when somebody is doing something wrong behind their back, it must be tempered with the overall desire to nurture the Sibling Relationships.

In our house when somebody tattled, the person who usually got in trouble was the tattletale. This seems dangerous, but when your children get old enough to understand what "tattletale" means, you can explain to them they have a responsibility to tell you in private if somebody is doing something truly dangerous, at which time you can handle the situation with the child who is guilty of the wrongdoing (making your best effort to protect the identity of your source). It's critical to make your children understand you won't punish their siblings for small infractions every time they tell on each other. They soon find out this is a way to push your buttons. It gives them a little power and gives them the satisfaction of getting somebody else in trouble. It just does more damage than good. You must try to help your children understand the differences between small infractions and the big ones.

Right to Privacy

A final piece of advice regarding siblings is to insist your children respect each other's privacy. Nobody should be allowed to storm into someone's bedroom without first knocking and asking permission. Nobody should be allowed to help themselves to their siblings' personal things such as favorite toys, a CD player, favorite pair of shoes or sweater without asking. Don't allow them to listen in on each other's private conversations, in person or on the telephone. Privacy becomes especially important to a child who is entering puberty. Every member of the family deserves a certain amount of privacy and should have the luxury of knowing their personal things, telephone conversations and space are theirs alone and not subject to unwanted intrusions.

A Happy Family

A family who fosters thoughtfulness and consideration among its members is a happy family. Brothers and sisters are more likely to form strong bonds, which will last a lifetime, if parents are cognizant of the importance of Sibling Relationships. Home should be a place where you are among the ones you trust, know you are respected and feel safe from the world. These are the things happy childhood memories are made of.

Fostering Sibling Relationships is the sixth essential element in Back to Basics discipline.

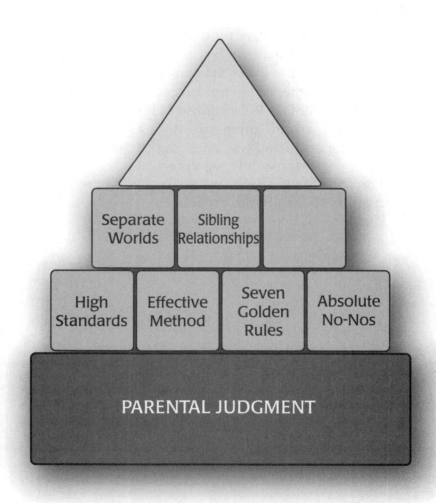

8

Home Environment

"Your home is the nest—make it safe,
warm, loving, nurturing and happy."

The Seventh Essential Element
in Back to Basics Discipline

Let's review one last time. We've covered High Standards, choosing the most Effective Method of discipline, the Seven Golden Rules, the Absolute No-Nos, Separate Worlds and Sibling Relationships. It's now time to put the frosting on the cake. Through my experience, and from what I learned from my parents, I've attempted to identify the things you can do for your children to create the right Home Environment.

The right Home Environment, which actually completes the overall discipline program, is about the way you run your household. It's about the influence you have on your children through the way you interact with your spouse and the way you interrelate with them. It's about teaching them by example and instilling your moral beliefs. It's letting them and everyone else know what your expectations are. It's going that extra mile.

Make Them Your Priority and Make Sure They Know It

This piece of advice is for working parents. Your children need to be told, and reminded often, they are your priority and are more important to you than your job or your career. Be mindful not to break promises to children because of your work and make yourself available to them as much as possible by telephone during the day. If you have a boss who won't allow it, get another job.

I had the unique experience of being a stay-at-home mom for about eight years, then working full-time outside of the home for about 16 years. I know first-hand the pressures and guilt of the working mom. Notwithstanding the pressures and guilt, you should do this one thing: make sure your children know they are more important to you than your job. You must put them first and they must know it. Whenever they call you while you are at work—drop everything else and talk to them. Don't rush the conversation; don't be upset because they called. Make them feel like they made your day just by calling you.

I had one exception to this rule. My children were not allowed to call me to settle any of their fights. They tried it once or twice and it didn't work. I not only refused to help, but I told them if they did it again I would just hang up, but if they called to tell me they got an "A" on a test or to tell me they needed help on a project, that was just fine. I even went so far as to make sure I was paged if I got a call from one of my children. My manager and my co-workers knew my children were important to me. They also knew I would quit work if I was required to deny my children's phone calls.

98

At work I was known as the "first person out the door at quitting time." People would try to make me feel guilty about it, but it never worked. The most important people in my life were waiting for me at home. I would be crazy to spend one extra minute at work just to avoid a few raised eyebrows. At five-thirty, I was outta there.

I would use my vacation time to stay home the first week of school each year. It always seemed like a time everyone needed to be "mommed" a little more, especially when they were in elementary school. By staying home the first week of school, I could be sure they got into their routines in the morning. I would also be there to hear all about their new teachers when they got home. After about a week, everyone was back in the routine and I felt better about going back to work.

Routine

Stability and a sense of security and predictability, through adherence to daily routines, make home a familiar and safe place for children. Routine should be part of every child's life beginning at birth. We know infants are more content when they have a regular feeding and sleeping schedule, but it shouldn't stop there. I made a priority of establishing routines at home for the kids. The routine of getting up and getting ready for school was the same every morning, the whole ritual of dinner and the chores they participated in after dinner were the same every night and bedtime was the same every night. Of course, there were the occasional exceptions, but most of the time the kids knew what to expect.

Sometimes, life deals us unanticipated change. As an example, I went to work when April, the youngest, was one year old after being a stay-at-home mom for eight years. It was supposed to be a part-time, temporary arrangement, but it turned out to be a full-time job which lasted for sixteen years. We decided John should move his office home so at least one of us was there for the kids every day.

It was a complete role reversal for us, which we all adjusted to better than I imagined. John was there when the kids came home from school and saw to it chores were done and homework was completed. He did the laundry, grocery shopping and cooking. Most importantly, he continued to maintain structure and routine in the home. His style was a little different than mine, but the rules were the same. I believe that's why the kids didn't seem to be affected by the change.

In cases of divorce, parents tend to feel guilty and understandably want to make everybody feel better. As a result, they change routines and ease up on discipline. As tempting as it is, it's a huge mistake. What children need, especially in divorce situations, is security. Changing routines and rules will upset them unnecessarily. Whatever your situation, if there is major change beyond your control, you will make life a little less scary for your kids by being consistent in daily routines and discipline.

Role Modeling

Show your children the best example of a husband-wife relationship. Demonstrate affection, admiration and respect for each other. Mothers and fathers are the natural role models for their children. Just by being around you so much, they pick up your mannerisms, your laugh and your sense of humor. Boys learn how to be good husbands by watching Dad. Daughters learn how to be good wives by watching Mom. It doesn't take a lot of effort to show your affection and respect for each other—it's the little things. My dad, every single night, would always thank my mother for the dinner she had cooked. I still remember seeing him wad up his napkin, throw it on the plate and say, "That was so good, Mom, thanks."

John always made a big deal out of my coming home from work. The house had to be clean and dinner had to be ready. He made a big deal out of a lot of things on my behalf. My birthday and Mother's Day were always big events. The celebrating started weeks ahead of time when he would engage the kids in teasing me about how many shopping days there were before my birthday. He made no bones about the fact I was important to him in front of the kids.

If fathers treat mothers with respect, sons will, in turn, treat women with respect. Daughters will know how a wife and mother should be treated. Since my husband always treated me with respect, I knew Jeanine, Janette and April would be able to recognize whether or not they were being treated properly. Anything less than the way I was treated would sound a silent alarm deep in their souls, and with one of them it actually did. Knowing her dad never treated her mom the way one young man had begun to treat her after about a year of dating, she knew she had to break it off. I am convinced to this day, had she married that particular young man, it would have been a mistake. I know Ken also gained his expectations for a relationship and beliefs of how he should be treated through our example.

Moral Values

Make it a priority to teach your children your moral values every chance you get. We seized every opportunity to bolster lessons in morality. Subtle approaches seemed to be more effective than lecturing, especially when they reached their teens. Watching television with your kids in the evening provides abundant opportunity. Many television shows deal with issues such as smoking, drug and alcohol abuse, sexual promiscuity, teen pregnancy and birth control. When the kids were old enough to watch programming like this, we would watch with them and John and I would verbalize our opinions about those issues. We would encourage discussions after the show about people we knew who did certain things and what happened to them. Sometimes, using hypothetical examples, we would let them know we disapproved of certain behaviors which might be acceptable by society in general, but not by us. Since none of the discussions were directed at them, rather at a fictitious character on television or somebody we knew, it created an environment where they felt free to participate in the discussions. It made them think about real-life issues. It contributed to their ability to analyze important life decisions and possible outcomes. It helped them develop critical thinking skills. Moreover, a lot of our moral values sank in.

Dinnertime

My mom had a special rule about dinnertime—it was a punishment-free zone. She insisted dinnertime, when we all sat around the table together, was going to be a happy time. After I was grown and out of the house she explained to me that my dad had gotten into the habit of using dinnertime to scold us kids for anything he happened to think of at the time. She put a stop to it by having a talk with him and getting him to agree dinnertime should be a pleasant experience for everyone. After that, my dad never broke the dinnertime rule. In fact, looking back, I can see he made an earnest effort to make us laugh by telling us funny stories and jokes at the dinner table. It was a special time.

A happy family dinner is such a fond childhood memory of mine, I naturally wanted that for my children. I enforced Mom's dinnertime rules and my children enjoyed a punishment-free zone. Dinnertime is the perfect opportunity for the whole family to escape the rigor and business of life and just be a family. When scolding and lecturing are not allowed, free sharing of thoughts, opinions and expression find a safe place to flourish. You actually get to know your children and they get to know you.

Great Expectations

Family life in the Matson household was very similar to the one in which I grew up. We were strict parents. Nobody got away with anything. We were tough on the kids when they were young, and as a result we got to enjoy them as teenagers. I used to hear people say things to me like, "Just wait until they're teenagers," as if they were predicting my life would be a living hell when my children became teens. I would hear people express how they dreaded their kids becoming teenagers as if they expected their kids to suddenly become possessed by evil spirits and make everyone's life miserable. I guess in some cases, what they feared actually did happen. Was it a self-fulfilling prophecy?

If you expect kids to be a certain way, they will rise to the occasion. Since I raised my kids the way I was raised, I was confident this wasn't going to happen to my family, and it didn't. I also was mindful of things I would say around them. I was forthcoming about loving teenagers. I would say things like, "I don't know what you mean, I love teenagers. They're so energetic and full of life." This always shocked people, but it was the truth. I never wanted my kids to hear me say I dreaded their teen years. They would have thought I expected them to be awful. It was the exact opposite. I expected them to be spectacular and made no bones about it. They did not disappoint me.

We always received compliments from the kids' teachers. Each year, there was a parent-teacher conference for each of the children a month or two after school started. It was an opportunity for parents and teachers to discuss how the child was doing in class and to discuss any problems, if there were any. I am not exaggerating when I say, at every parent-teacher conference I attended for my children, the teacher always remarked about what a well-behaved student my child was, and it usually didn't stop there. The teacher would usually ask how I did it. I always responded by saying I had high expectations for my kids and anything less would simply not be acceptable.

John and I believe if you have high expectations about children, they will rise to the occasion. Therefore, it makes sense to have high expectations. This doesn't mean your expectations should be unreasonable. I'm talking about expecting kids to behave and do well in school. Helping them to be the best they can be is done several ways. First, directly through the consistent application of discipline and correcting bad behavior when it occurs and, less directly, in the way you talk to them and about them. Be careful what you say—everything they hear, especially from a parent, becomes programmed in them like a computer. When they hear you saying repeatedly they are good, polite, special, outstanding kids, they believe you and those things become a part of who *they* believe they are. It helps to shape a positive self-image.

Take every opportunity to say something positive about your kids! Do it in subtle, unexpected ways giving it authenticity. We often referred to our children as "the Matson kids," as if they belonged to a prestigious and special group. They would hear us say things to each other like, "I wonder if Mrs. Hunt knows how lucky she is to have another Matson kid in her class this year," or, "The Matson kids are the best, the smartest and the most well-behaved kids at that school." We would say it to each other as if nobody else was in the room, but we knew they were listening. This instilled a sense of pride and belonging in that they were Matson kids. It also instilled in them the image of a Matson kid was a positive one which they needed to live up to. Inasmuch as kids need their individuality, they also need a sense of belonging.

The Power of Your Smile

A smile is a little thing, but so powerful. One of the loving things my mother always did was smile when I walked into the room. She didn't have to say a word.

Mom's smile was always the most genuine welcome I could ever hope for. It just made me feel good. If I'd had a bad day, it was instantly forgotten. When I became a mother I looked back and remembered the positive impact those warm welcomes had on my sense of worthiness and significance. I have always made it a point to smile when my children enter the room—each one is the light of my life.

Negative Images

One of the most important pieces of advice I have is for those who are divorced and have children. Be mindful of the way you talk about your former-spouse in front of the children. The harm you do to children by saying negative things about their mother or father is irreparable. They get a sense of who they are from their perceptions of their parents. A little boy doesn't need to hear his father is a liar, a drunk or a cheat. It is hurtful to kids—don't do it and don't let anybody else do it.

Keep Disagreements Private

My parents never argued or fought in front of us children. I naturally assumed everyone's parents were like mine until I went on a weekend trip with a friend to her family's beach house when I was about eleven years old. What sounded like so much fun turned out to be a miserable time. The first day was fine. It only took an hour to get there and, after unpacking, we played on the beach all day. Later that night, things took a turn for the worst. My friend, her sister and I bunked down in a small bedroom next to the bedroom where her parents were. The wall was very thin; at least thin enough for us to hear their parents fighting. It was awful. I had never heard grown-ups talk to each other like that. I was so frightened, I just pulled the covers over my head. My friend and her sister just shrugged as if to say, "Welcome to our world." From that point on I couldn't wait to go home. I don't remember the rest of the weekend because I was so focused on getting home where I felt safe. I never forgot the feeling of being a small child hearing adults fighting. It was then that I realized how lucky I was my parents didn't fight or, if they did, I never knew about it. I never accepted an invitation from this particular friend again, not even to go over to her house and play, which was just across the street.

Don't ever fight or argue in front of your children. Moving the argument or fight in the next room is futile because they can still hear it. It is so damaging it should be considered a form of child abuse. Children who are exposed to their parents' fights are insecure, tense and fearful. They are robbed of their self-esteem and they learn fighting with your spouse is normal behavior. There's no excuse for it and it should not be done.

Your Home is Your Nest

There are so many things you can do to create an environment your children can thrive in. Start with the following tips:

- Make sure your children know they are your priority.
- Create a safe, predictable environment through daily routines.

- Show your children the best example of a husband-wife relationship.
- Teach children moral values whenever you can.
- Make dinnertime a punishment-free zone.
- Broadcast your high expectations.
- Be generous with your approving smile.
- Tell them over and over how wonderful they are.
- Keep disagreements private.

You can be creative and add many more great parenting tips to this collection, as I am sure you will. Your home is the nest. Make it safe, warm, loving, nurturing and happy. A happy, healthy Home Environment is the seventh essential element in Back to Basics discipline.

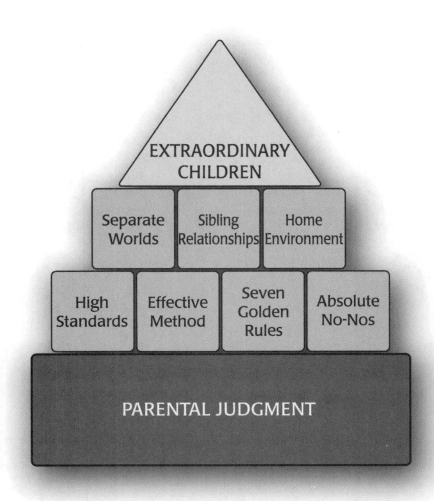

9

Putting it All Together

*" . . . you can expect to receive
compliments on a daily basis about
what good children you have."*

We've now covered all seven essential elements:

High Standards

Effective Method

Seven Golden Rules

Absolute No-Nos

Separate Worlds

Sibling Relationships

Home Environment

Each single element is a power tool for parenting, but put them all together with your parental judgment and you have a combined synergism which garners results unmatched in the world of parenting today.

Be forewarned, you will need an enormous amount of stubborn courage in today's permissive environment to actually assert yourself as a parent by using Back to

Basics discipline. It will be difficult because you will, no doubt, encounter criticism such as the criticism my mother received from family members when she was warned her children wouldn't love her when they grew up. You will be scoffed, scorned and subjected to countless patronizing remarks. . . if you are not following the herd, you are just not doing it right. The funny thing is, you will actually encounter such disapproval from people at the exact moment your children are behaving and theirs are not.

On the other hand, you can expect to receive compliments on a daily basis about what good children you have. Disciplined children are noticed and people just can't resist letting you know about it.

I recall on many occasions people would acknowledge what well-behaved children I had but it would be followed by a statement like, "Just wait until they get into high school, that's when they turn on you," or, "Just wait until they are teenagers, they'll get lazy and their grades will drop." When that happened I would just ignore the negative comment, and try to suppress the Mona Lisa-like smile on my face so as not to look too smug and confident.

Another comment my mother and I often got was, "You're so lucky your kids are good." My mother's response was always, "Luck had nothing to do with it." She resented the way people tried to take away her accomplishment by saying it was luck, when in actuality it was commitment on her part to raise great kids.

In addition to outside pressures and comments from other people, this kind of discipline program requires parents stay the course. You must not backslide. You cannot let something go one day because you don't feel like getting up or you are too busy—you have too much invested and it could be lost just by not being consistent (Golden Rule 2).

There are going to be days you feel like you are the mom from hell because you have done nothing but discipline a child all day. There will be days you will cry and have doubts and wonder if it is all worth it but it won't be like that every day. If you are consistent with discipline, and if you win every power struggle, your children will respect your authority, which is the cornerstone of success. Keep in mind discipline is about the child and the important lessons in life he needs to learn in order to develop strong character. Remember, discipline is not about *anger*, it's about *love*.

Consider this a lifestyle change. Think about my mother's house and how it was more than discipline, it was the environment she maintained. My mother is the perfect role model for anyone who wants to be a respected and effective parent. She is my mother, however, I am willing to share her with anyone who needs a strong parental role model.

Your efforts will be rewarded. Through this discipline program your children will learn they're not entitled to everything on demand. They will learn the virtues of patience, understanding, kindness and consideration. They will be good students, good teens and extraordinary adults. They will enjoy loving relationships with their siblings and they will have happy childhood memories. They will be *extraordinary*.

Back to Basics discipline is not an experiment or an untested new theory or popular trend. It's definitely not politically correct. However, this discipline program works. It's based on a few simple undeniable truths about children. They crave discipline. They actually love and respect the parents who provide them the discipline they crave. They respond to discipline favorably by learning important lessons in life and, having done so, their capacity to enjoy life is endless.

By reading this book, you have taken the first step toward raising great kids. After your children are grown and they start having children of their own, don't drop the ball, pass along the secrets of Back to Basics discipline to them like my mother did for me. My hope is for this to be the beginning of a great tradition of raising extraordinary children in your family which continues for endless generations.

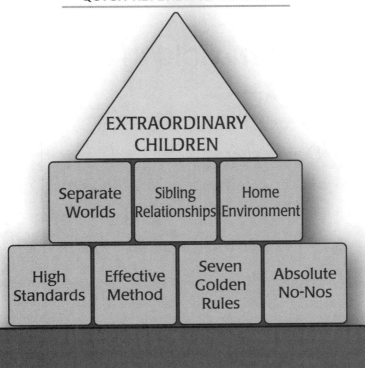

Back to Basics
DISCIPLINE
QUICK REFERENCE GUIDES

EXTRAORDINARY
CHILDREN

Separate
Worlds

Sibling
Relationships

Home
Environment

High
Standards

Effective
Method

Seven
Golden
Rules

Absolute
No-Nos

PARENTAL JUDGMENT

Back to Basics
DISCIPLINE
QUICK REFERENCE GUIDES

Seven Golden Rules

1. *Start early*
2. *Be consistent*
3. *Don't delay*
4. *Never punish when you're angry*
5. *Always follow through with a threat*
6. *Never apologize, explain or negotiate*
7. *Maintain a united front*

Absolute No-Nos

Disobedience

Disrespect

Temper

Dishonesty

Aggression

INDEX

Give the Gift of
Back to Basics Discipline
to Your Friends and Colleagues

CHECK YOUR LEADING BOOKSTORE OR ORDER HERE

❑ **YES**, I want _____ copies of *Back to Basics Discipline: A Program to Raise Extraordinary Children* at $16.95 each, plus $4.95 shipping per book (CA residents please add $1.23 sales tax per book). Canadian orders must be accompanied by a postal money order in U.S. funds. Allow 15 days for delivery.

❑ **YES**, I am interested in having Janet Campbell Matson speak or give a seminar to my company, association, school, or organization. Please send information.

My check or money order for $_____ is enclosed.

Name _____

Organization _____

Address _____

City/State/Zip _____

Phone_____ E-mail _____

Please make your check payable and return to:
Bee Good Books
2060-D Avenida Los Arboles, #338
Thousand Oaks, CA 91362

Or Order Online at
www.BackToBasicsDiscipline.com